The Busy Person's Meal Planner

A Beginner's Guide to
Healthy Meal Planning and Meal Prep

LAURA LIGOS, RDN, CSSD

BLUE·STAR
PRESS

Published by Blue Star Press
PO Box 8835, Bend, OR 97708
contact@bluestarpress.com
www.bluestarpress.com

Disclaimer: This book is for informational and
educational purposes. It is not intended to diagnose,
treat, cure, or prevent any disease. Please consult your
healthcare provider before starting or modifying any
diet, exercise, or healthcare program.

Interior Design by Chris Ramirez and Rhoda Wong
Cover Design by Megan Kesting and Rhoda Wong

ISBN: 9781950968398

Printed in Thailand

10 9 8 7 6 5 4 3 2 1

Contents

Introduction

When you hear the phrase "meal plan," what comes to mind? If you're like a lot of people, those words probably conjure up a vision of some wonderfully laid-out calendar that has every last meal and snack planned for the days ahead. You might imagine someone who spends their Sunday afternoons cooking meals for the week and then putting perfectly sized portions into their freezer for themselves and their family. Then, of course, that person follows their meal plan to a T without any mistakes...and definitely without slipping up and ordering takeout or delivery.

While this vision of meal planning might be idealistic, it's certainly not realistic. As a registered dietitian, I regularly work with clients who come to me hoping for some magic trick or special secret to meal planning. They figure there must be one "right way" to do it, and that they need to follow that plan carefully if they want it to work. What they're always surprised to learn is that I don't have a trick up my sleeve. In fact, I don't believe in following any gimmicks when it comes to eating.

What I always tell them is that the typical person is too busy for a "perfect" plan. If you're juggling a demanding job, an active family, or both, you know that no two weeks look the same. What you need is a no-nonsense guide that teaches you how to make meal planning more accessible and enjoyable in your life. You need a plan that's easy to learn, easy to do, and easy to maintain. You need something that's flexible enough to suit your individual life and needs. You need a plan that you can follow without feeling stressed, and also without feeling shame or guilt if some days don't go as planned.

I designed *The Busy Person's Meal Planner* to give you a guide to practical meal planning and to offer easy answers to the age-old question, "what's for dinner?" In this book, I share the five basic meal-planning steps that I teach all my clients, as well as other tips and tools to make the process of food prep and cooking simpler for you. I also share more than 50 recipes that are easy to cook, and tasty enough that you'll want to prepare them again and again. These recipes are also easily modifiable depending on your taste preferences or dietary needs.

In the back of this book, you'll find a weekly meal planner and grocery list notepad that you can use to map out your meals and jot down what you need to pick up at the store. Hang the meal plan on the fridge for everyone in your household to see, then tear out the grocery list and bring it along with you to the supermarket (or take a photo of it so that it's stored on your phone, if that's more your style).

Once you get the hang of meal planning, you'll feel better knowing that you don't have to stress about having always-empty cupboards; you don't have to feel lost navigating the grocery store aisles; and you don't have to spend time or money that you don't have trying to get healthy meals on your dinner table each week.

So if you're ready to get started, let's dive into some simple meal-planning basics to give you a fresh perspective on what meal planning is, and how you can fit it into your busy life. 🍽

Meal Planning 101

WHAT EXACTLY *IS* MEAL PLANNING?

Meal planning is a strategy to help you plan your meals out ahead of time, and obtain the ingredients you need to make those meals for the week. It's not necessarily about prepping all those meals ahead of time (although if that works for you, by all means do it!). It's simply a roadmap for your week so you don't have to open your kitchen cabinets every night and wonder, "What the heck am I going to eat?"

> A meal plan is a lot like having a to-do list. Not everyone does it the same way, but everyone is better off having one.

A meal plan will help you save time and money. It will also help you prioritize your health goals and stay on track for the long term. The goal of meal planning is not to overwhelm you. Just like anything else in life, it will take practice for you to feel confident doing it. But over time, you will find that the act of meal planning can seamlessly fit into your life—and be stress-free.

MEAL PLAN a tool to help you figure out and schedule out what you will eat over the course of a week.

WHY MEAL PLANNING IS IMPORTANT

Meal planning is a key component of a healthy lifestyle. Why? Because it lays the groundwork for actually getting healthy meals on your plate. After all, a dream without a plan is just a wish. A meal plan helps make the process of healthy eating more efficient and effective. In other words, it ensures that you'll actually do it.

While we can certainly wing it and hope for the best, a plan will help you actually follow through with healthy eating. And the best plans are adaptable. I see clients who feel like they need to track every last bite of food, only to fail at that and, lacking a plan, end up eating whatever is in front of them or most convenient. Most diets fail, and it's not because the individual didn't try hard enough; it's because the diet wasn't realistic or flexible enough for their needs over the long run.

The solution? Make a plan to ensure that you are paying attention to your health and the food that goes on your plate, without feeling like you can't indulge from time to time. (Because after all, pizza night should absolutely be a thing—and can even be planned ahead of time!) Meal planning is a more flexible way to prioritize your health, and can help make a healthy lifestyle feel less restrictive and more manageable in the long term.

As I said before, there is no perfect way to meal plan because everyone's appetite, taste, and needs change over time. Some weeks you might make a little too much food. Other weeks you may not make enough. Remember, it's OK. You're going to learn by doing this over and over again.

MY APPROACH TO MEAL PLANNING

After working with hundreds of clients, the five-step method that follows is what I have found to be the easiest approach to meal planning. It's easy to start, and it's easy to maintain. This isn't about following strict rules because let's be honest: When has following some super-specific eating regimen ever worked for you in the past? The goal here is to eat in a way that is incredibly realistic, flexible, and manageable.

Meal planning takes some getting used to, but once you learn the steps, you will feel confident and comfortable following it weekly. This process is meant to help you get food on your plate with ease, and without feeling overwhelmed or spending too much time on meal prep.

The steps laid out on the following pages are my go-to process for meal-planning success. Use them to help you get into the swing of things, then as you get more comfortable, feel free to combine steps, or skip ones that you feel are no longer necessary for you.

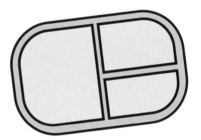

NOTE

WHY I WILL NEVER PROMOTE A DIET

As a dietitian, I like to think of myself as a non-biased food expert and enthusiast. For that reason, I do not believe that there is a one-size-fits-all way to eat. Some people feel better when they eat more meat, while others prefer to follow a plant-based diet. Some opt for a gluten-free approach, while others have no problem with wheat. Many people want a healthy balance of everything. The great thing about meal planning is that there is room for everyone at the table. We can all plan meals that help to meet our needs and our taste buds. You don't have to fit inside a diet structure in order to be healthy. And frankly, most people would be healthier and feel better if they just listened to their bodies instead of an arbitrary set of rules. So to sum it up: no diets for this dietitian. Can I get a "heck, yeah?!"

PRE-MEAL PLANNING EXERCISE: FIND YOUR FAVORITE RECIPES

Before you get too far down the meal-planning rabbit hole, I want you to start by making a list of 10 of your favorite go-to dinner recipes. Create a file on your phone or computer, or print out the recipes so they are easily accessible. This exercise is intended to reduce stress by building an arsenal of recipes you can refer to whenever you are planning your meals for the week. We're starting with recipes you already love or feel comfortable making because, again, I want meal planning to be something that fits naturally into your life.

"Go-to recipes" should be ones that:

- You've tried before and enjoyed
- You feel confident making
- You know will satisfy most people in your household

They should also have the three main components of a nutritious (and delicious) meal:

Protein
There should always be a source of protein on your plate. Why? Because it keeps you full the longest and leaves you feeling satisfied. Aim for 20 grams of protein or more per person per meal whenever possible.

Fruits/Vegetables
Each meal should have some type of natural color in the form of a fruit and/or a vegetable. Not sure what to add? Check out what's in season!

Flavor
Adding spices, herbs, citrus juices or zest, or even a sprinkle of cheese as a finishing touch will help ensure that your recipes are flavorful. After all, you want each of your go-to recipes to be so good that you'll want to eat them over and over again.

If you're having trouble coming up with 10 recipes that you know fit into these categories, don't fret. That's why I've included popular, easy-to-make, dinner recipes starting on page 64. Flip through the pages and find some meals that sound good to you, then add them to your list. As you get comfortable with meal planning over time, feel free to add new go-to recipes to your list as well. The goal is to give you plenty of healthy ideas when you sit down to make your weekly menu.

Now, it's time to get to work on that meal plan. We're going to start by planning just a few dinners for the week (or maybe only one, if that sounds less intimidating to you). Don't worry about breakfast or lunch just yet. Once you've gotten the hang planning your dinners for the week, then you can move on to adding your favorite breakfast and lunch options to your recipe list and planning those meals for the week as well.

1

survey the scene

The first step to meal planning for the week is taking a look at what ingredients you already have available. You can save money, time, and energy by using what you already have on hand. When you survey the scene (a.k.a. your kitchen), take notes on which ingredients you've already got, and which ones you may need to stock up on at the grocery store.

Take inventory. Check all the locations in and around your house where you store food. After all, it's easy to forget about something when it's way in the back of the fridge. That forgetfulness is usually what leads us to pick up more than we need when we're shopping the aisles.

Take a look at the following places:

- Pantry
- Cabinets
- Refrigerator
- Freezer
- Any additional storage, refrigerators, freezers, etc.

Check expiration dates. As you're surveying the scene, take note of any food that will expire soon, and try to prioritize those items to use in your meal plan for the week. Doing so will reduce food waste and help you rotate through items in a more cost-effective and efficient way.

2

mind the sales and seasons

After you've assessed what ingredients you already have or need to use soon, it's time to look at what ingredients are on sale and in season at your local grocery stores. Eating healthy doesn't have to be expensive, and finding ways to save money is a great way to shop! Here are a few helpful places to look for sales.

- Store flyers and websites
- Store-specific apps, such as Target, Walmart, and Amazon Fresh
- Grocery-saving apps, such as Checkout 51, Ibotta, and SnipSnap

Knowing what produce is in season can also help your budget and your taste buds. To see what's in season in your area, check out a website like www.seasonalfoodguide.org. is usually less expensive and more abundant, nutritious, and tasty.

 NOTE

What's in season will depend where you live, so this is just a general guide. As a rule of thumb, what is most abundant and placed front and center in the produce section of your grocery store will most likely be what is in season. To see what's in season in your area, check out a website like www.seasonalfoodguide.org.

SEASONAL PRODUCE GUIDE

Here are a few examples of what is typically in season throughout the year:

fall

Apples
Bananas
Beets
Bell Peppers
Broccoli
Brussels Sprouts
Cabbage
Carrots
Cauliflower
Celery
Collard Greens
Cranberries
Garlic
Ginger
Grapes
Green Beans
Kale
Kiwi
Lemons
Lime
Lettuce
Mangoes
Mushrooms
Onions
Parsnips
Pears
Peas
Pineapples
Potatoes
Radishes
Raspberries
Rutabaga
Spinach
Sweet Potatoes
Yams
Swiss Chard
Turnips
Winter Squash

winter

Apples
Avocados
Bananas
Beets
Brussels Sprouts
Cabbage
Carrots
Celery
Collard Greens
Grapefruit
Kale
Kiwi
Leeks
Lemons
Limes
Onions
Oranges
Parsnips
Pears
Pineapples
Potatoes
Pumpkins
Rutabagas
Sweet Potatoes
Yams
Swiss Chard
Turnips
Winter Squash

spring

Apples
Apricots
Avocados
Bananas
Broccoli
Cabbage
Carrots
Celery
Collard Greens
Garlic
Kale
Kiwi
Lemons/Limes
Lettuce
Mushrooms
Onions
Peas
Pineapples
Radishes
Rhubarb
Spinach
Strawberries
Swiss Chard
Turnips

summer

Apples
Apricots
Avocados
Bananas
Beets
Bell Peppers
Blackberries
Blueberries
Cantaloupe
Carrots
Celery
Cherries
Corn
Cucumbers
Eggplant
Garlic
Green Beans
Honeydew Melon
Lemons
Limes
Lima Beans
Mangoes
Okra
Peaches
Plums
Raspberries
Strawberries
Summer Squash
Tomatillos
Tomatoes
Watermelon
Zucchini

Source: USDA.gov

3

make your menu

Now that you know what you have on hand, what's on sale, and what's in season, it's time to make your menu. Refer back to your list of go-to recipes and pick two to three that you want to prep for dinner this week, keeping any ingredients you know you want to use in mind. If this is already sounding overwhelming to you, then just start with one recipe. Remember, you want to start slowly and create a meal-planning process that is realistic, flexible, and easy to maintain.

As a reminder, we're starting with dinner before we start adding meal-prepped breakfasts and lunches to our menu. Dinner is usually the easiest meal to plan at first because we have the time, support, and motivation to make it. Plus, it's the meal your family is most likely to sit down and eat together.

Here's where to start:

- Write down which days you want to make those meals and eat those leftovers, then reserve the one or two days remaining for takeout or easy grab-and-go options. This way, pizza night won't derail your plans—it's already planned.

- Check over your menu and make sure each meal has the right mix of protein, colorful fruits and vegetables, carbs, and fat. See page 24 for more on building a quality, well-portioned plate.

4

make a list and get shopping

Now that you have a good idea of what you will be making, you need to determine what ingredients you need to pick up at the store. Since you've already done a great job surveying the scene in your kitchen, you should know what you do and don't need based on the recipes you have planned.

Use your recipes to write down your grocery list (remembering to increase the quantity of ingredients for any recipes you plan to double), and add anything else you need from around the house (soap, shampoo, dog food, etc.). This is also a good time to check the Pantry Staples list on page 109 to see if there are any essential cooking items like oils or spices that you need to restock.

Now it's time to go grocery shopping. This can be overwhelming to many, but going in with a plan and a list of what you need should make it less stressful. I recommend trying to limit your trip to one or two stores to be more efficient.

When you get to the store, do not worry if you can't find everything on your list. Instead, think about what would make a great substitute for whatever you can't find. For instance, your store may be out of zucchini, so go for yellow summer squash instead. If all else fails, use your phone and search online for a good substitute. You can improvise and still stay on track to make the tasty meals on your menu.

When you are about to check out, double-check your shopping cart. Make sure you got everything on your list, and that you didn't let too many off-list items slip in there. While it can be tempting to shop off-list, this can cause more waste and confusion as the week goes on. Just remember, we're all human, so things like chips and cookies will slip into the cart from time to time. But planning will help reduce spontaneity in your shopping and build your confidence when you go to the store.

If you find going into the store to be too much for you, you can also try ordering your groceries online for delivery or pick up. This simple convenience can actually help you streamline your process and prevent you from buying things you don't need. Some stores' apps and websites even save your previous orders, which makes it easy to just pick items from the last time you made those meals. If ordering your groceries reduces stress and saves time, then trust me: it's well worth the money.

5

prep your meals

Congratulations—you should now be the proud owner of a week-long meal plan and all the groceries you need to get started! Making a plan and obtaining all the needed ingredients can sometimes be the hardest part of this process, so give yourself a pat on the back. Now you're ready to schedule some time to prep the food you plan to eat all week. After all, a plan without any execution equals no food on your actual plate!

First, let's back up for one second. What does it mean to meal prep? Many people think that meal prep involves a lot of plastic containers all filled with each day's meals. While that certainly can be true if cooking ahead works for you, don't think that it's the only way to meal prep. When I talk about meal prep, I mean the process of getting food ready to be eaten. That includes things like pre-washing our vegetables, chopping and slicing of main ingredients, pre-cooking a batch of chicken or rice, or even combining spices for a dish ahead of time.

This prep may happen each day (i.e., an hour before we eat) or it can happen days beforehand (i.e., chop the veggies ahead of time so they are ready for that week's dinners). It may also include making full meals ahead of time like casseroles, soups, chili, etc. and storing them in the refrigerator or freezer to reheat for later. There isn't any one right way to meal prep. Feel free to experiment and find which ways work best for you and your family.

Here are a few options:

- Prep daily. If it fits in your schedule, there is no reason you can't prep daily and simply make your dinner from start to finish when you get home from work.

- Prep the day before. Getting some items ready for dinner the day or night before gives you less to worry about the following day. When you're ready to move on to meal planning breakfasts and lunches, it can also be helpful to prepare these meals the night before.

- Prep for the week ahead. Some people love doing their week's worth of meal prep all at once. Set aside two to three hours on a weekend day and get busy. This can be time consuming on that day, but it makes the rest of the week fly by.

- Prep a few hours a week for a few days at a time. Sometimes splitting up the prep, such as prepping every Sunday and Wednesday, can make for a shorter prep period and less active cooking days.

There is no easy button here, but if you schedule your meal prep, it is more likely to happen. So put it on your calendar and get to work.

~

MEAL PLANNING BREAKFASTS, LUNCHES, AND SNACKS

Once you've been meal planning your dinners for a few weeks and feel confident in the process, it's time to forge ahead. It's easy to think that breakfast and lunch will just plan themselves, but if you're being honest with yourself, you know that when you don't plan them, they become a free-for-all.

Lunch

It's important that we don't skimp on lunch! We want to fuel ourselves for the day, not famish ourselves, so do yourself a favor and pack a protein- and fiber-rich meal. Doing so will give you the energy you need and set you up for success throughout the day.

Let's start by adding some lunches that you love to your go-to recipe list. Not sure where to start? Find some easy and delicious lunch recipes on page 46. Identify five to ten recipes that fill you up (remember that protein), have some color from fiber-rich fruits and veggies, and make you excited to pack your lunch.

If you're like most people, you've probably gone on kicks of packing your lunch religiously, only to then never pack it at all. The goal here is to make lunch a manageable part of meal planning. Just as you did with dinner, start by planning one to two lunch options you can eat throughout your week and do that for a few weeks until you get comfortable. You can even pencil in days when you know you'll want to grab takeout instead.

NOTE

If you work from home, this process still applies to you. Just because you don't travel to work doesn't mean you do not "go" to work, so approach your lunchtime meal planning just as you would if you were going into an office. Figure out what you want to eat ahead of time, and maybe even make it and pack it the night before.

Breakfast

Once you've successfully planned both lunch and dinner for a few weeks, you're ready to move on to breakfast. Revisit your list of recipes and add five to ten go-to breakfasts that you know and love. (See page 30 for some fun ideas). Breakfast does not have to be boring—it should be substantial and enjoyable. Ideally, you want 20 to 30 grams of protein, a source of fiber (i.e., fruits, veggies, nuts, or seeds), and of course, carbs and fat.

Let's start with planning one or two breakfast options for the week. While you may want to pick more options than that, remember the goal is to be realistic and make your plan manageable over the long run. Variety sounds nice in theory, but it's going to be a lot harder to maintain. Can you imagine having to buy and make seven different breakfasts instead of one to two? Just keep it simple!

DON'T FORGET SNACKS!

We often let our hunger and corporate marketing dictate the snacks we put in our grocery carts. Instead, let's plan for our snacks.

Usually, I recommend having three to five options handy in your pantry or fridge; however, if you like to have more on hand, that's fine too. Just pick options that won't go bad in one week, like nuts and seeds. To keep it healthy, plan out snacks that have protein and some fiber to fill you up.

A few ideas for easy snacks:

- Energy bites

- Apples and peanut butter

- Grapes and cashews

- Rice cakes with peanut butter and berries

- Greek yogurt with berries and mixed nuts

- A cheese stick and a banana

- Carrot sticks with hummus

- Celery and peanut butter

- A meat stick or jerky

- Hard-boiled eggs and an apple

- Cottage cheese and peaches or pineapple

Refer to page 84 for a few easy-to-make snack recipes.

Food Quality & Quantity

When we start meal planning regularly and focusing more on eating healthy, we often want to know exactly what we should be eating and how much. While the answer seems like it should be simple, it really does depend on your individual dietary desires and needs.

As I tell all of my clients, we are looking for progress, not perfection, when it comes to our nutrition. Focusing on what you eat (quality) and how much (quantity) is important, which is why I want to break these two ideas down to the basics to make it easier for you.

Take the tips from this section and apply them to your meal-planning process little by little. Both quality and quantity can impact your health, which is why I want to show you how to make small changes over a period of time so that you can improve the food you eat and make it easier to keep up a healthy lifestyle.

WHAT IS QUALITY AND WHY DOES IT MATTER?

Quality is what your food consists of, where it comes from, how it's processed, and what micronutrients (i.e., vitamins, minerals, etc.) it contains. Higher-quality food is usually minimally processed and includes valuable nutrients that add to your overall health.

Focusing on the quality of your food is more important to me than counting numbers. After all, when we start getting bogged down with calories, that's when things get stressful. Instead, try to focus on where your food came from, whether it has any vitamins or minerals in it, and whether it will make you feel good. These are the more important parts of nutrition, in my opinion. If you look through all the research and diets out there, the one thing everyone can agree upon is that we need to eat more fruits and vegetables. Why? Because fruits and veggies are real, whole, and unprocessed foods. They contain the most high-quality components—ones that have been around for generations. That means our body knows how to digest, absorb, and utilize them.

In my experience, it's also rather hard to over-consume quality, mostly unprocessed ingredients. Let's take a potato, for example. When we bake a potato, we are more or less satisfied when we eat that potato and don't feel hungry afterward. However, the second we put that potato through a higher level of processing, say, in the form of potato chips, it becomes harder for us to pump the brakes on portion control.

Why? Because more often than not, the potatoes in those chips have been stripped of some of their original nutritional value. Now they also have added fats, salt, and sugar to make the chips more palatable. This is not to say you should never eat potato chips, but it's important to be aware that it's far easier to manage portion size with a higher-quality food (potato) than a lesser-quality food (potato chips).

I often tell my clients that when we are looking for quality food, we want to look for foods that are ingredients...not necessarily ones that have ingredients.

For example:
Potato = potato
Potato chip = potatoes + oil + salt

HOW TO SPOT QUALITY IN THE STORE

The concept of quality can seem simple at first, until you realize how much variation there is in the quality of foods at the store. As I tell my clients, I'd much rather you eat a vegetable in any way possible than not eat it at all. So if you are newer to cooking at home and haven't been eating a ton of real, quality food before now, start by adding vegetables and fruit in any form, and don't worry about the slight differences between quality (i.e., organic vs. conventional, or fresh vs. canned).

That being said, if you are further along in your food journey and want more clarification on what to look for in your food, here are some helpful tips:

Meat, *includes beef, bison, lamb, pork, venison*

WHAT TO LOOK FOR
Grass-fed. Ideally it is 100 percent grass-fed, meaning it was grass-fed and grass-finished, but even partly grass-fed is more desirable than conventionally-raised meat. You may even see a classification for "pasture-raised" for things like pork, which means the animal also had room to roam and graze.

WHAT DOES GRASS-FED MEAN?
It means that the animal had access to grass. Animals like cows are ruminants as well as herbivores, which means they prefer to eat grass over grain and tend to be healthier as a result of a grass-fed diet. This is not only better for the animals, but also means the meat from them is of higher nutritional value for you.

HOW TO BUDGET FOR GRASS-FED MEAT
Buy in bulk. When you see grass-fed meat on sale, stock up. You can also find a local animal share and split it with another family or two; this will reduce cost per pound.

Aim for ground meat. Ground meat tends to be cheaper per pound and thus easier on the budget.

Opt for leaner cuts. The leaner cuts of meat may seem more expensive, but you get more bang for your buck because you will not have to trim the fat or cook it off.

WHAT IF YOU CAN'T FIND GRASS-FED MEAT, OR STILL CAN'T AFFORD IT?
That's OK, don't panic. It's fine to eat food that isn't 100 percent the highest quality possible. Instead, consider reducing your red meat intake until you can find a higher quality, or buying leaner cuts of conventionally-raised meats. Leaner cuts tend to be higher quality, and since the antibiotics, hormones, and pesticides are stored in the fat, there will be less of them in a leaner cut, making it a better option overall. The recipes in this book were made using grass-fed meat whenever possible.

Poultry, *includes chicken, duck, turkey*

WHAT TO LOOK FOR:
Pasture-raised

WHAT DOES PASTURE-RAISED MEAN?
This means that the animals were raised outdoors year-round with access to shelter for protection from weather and predators. Chickens and turkeys, for example, are grazers and will eat pretty much anything. That's why allowing them space to move around and forage is a healthier option than having them cooped up in an overcrowded cage. When chickens are allowed to roam and graze freely, they

end up eating a diet that not only is healthier for them but also is healthier for us when we consume their meat. Pasture-raised animals have a lower percentage of fat and also higher omega 3s, which can help reduce our own inflammation—a win-win.

HOW TO BUDGET FOR PASTURE-RAISED POULTRY
Buy in bulk and when it's on sale. You can freeze poultry pretty easily, so stock up when you find a higher quality on sale.

Opt for leaner cuts. This will give you the most bang for your buck since you won't have to trim fat or cook it off.

WHAT TO DO IF YOU CAN'T FIND PASTURE-RAISED POULTRY?
Much like red meat, it makes more sense to buy the leaner cuts of lesser-quality poultry until you can find a higher-quality source. The recipes in this book used pasture-raised poultry or lean cuts of chicken whenever possible.

Fish, *includes fish and shellfish*

WHAT TO LOOK FOR:
Wild-caught, pole-caught, and/or sustainably fished

WHAT DOES FISH LABELING MEAN?
There are many resources like Monterey Bay Aquarium's Seafood Watch Guide that can show you the quality and safety of your fish. When it comes to fish, we want to shop for seafood that was raised in a healthy environment and watch out for unsafe mercury levels (mercury level warnings can be found in the Seafood Watch Guide mentioned above). This can look different for each type of fish, but generally shopping for one of the three categories above will ensure you're picking a healthier option.

TOP 10 FISH RECOMMENDATIONS

- Wild-caught salmon
- Chunk light/skipjack/albacore tuna
- Sardines
- Scallops
- Crab
- Shrimp
- Tilapia
- Mussels
- Black cod
- Pollock

WHAT IF YOU CAN'T FIND HIGH-QUALITY FISH?
Most fish are frozen or previously frozen, especially if you don't live where the fish was caught, to preserve the freshness and quality. So don't hesitate to buy frozen or even canned fish; it is still good quality!

Eggs

WHAT TO LOOK FOR:
Pasture-raised, cage-free, free-range, and/or organic

WHAT DOES EGG LABELING MEAN?
Usually, the labeling is referring to the environment in which the chickens were raised and the feed they were offered. Buy the best-quality eggs you can find in your area within your budget. You might be better off finding friends or local farmers with backyard chickens, as these will be the freshest source available to you and can help your local economy. Much like poultry, eggs have a higher nutrient content and more omega 3s when the chickens graze and have land to roam. Happier and healthier chickens mean more nutrient-dense eggs for you!

Fruits and Vegetables

WHAT TO LOOK FOR:
Fresh and in-season produce

When it comes to fruits and vegetables, fresh and in-season produce is best, but anything is better than nothing. In theory, a fresh vegetable is the best quality because it is fresher and less tampered with than the ones in a can or freezer bag. However, if you buy fresh vegetables and they just rot in your refrigerator, was it even worth it? Probably not. I recommend trying to stick to fresh whenever possible, but you can use frozen fruits and veggies when necessary for convenience and to avoid food waste. When all else fails, canned fruits and vegetables are an OK option; just look for a brand that is stored in its own juices or water and not in a bath of unwanted ingredients and sugar.

If you have the budget to buy organic produce and/or from a local farm, great. If not, it's not the end of the world. Just wash your fruits and vegetables with water and call it good. Remember, eating any fruit or vegetable is better than none at all!

Dairy

WHAT TO LOOK FOR:
Grass-fed or low in fat

Much like meat, you will want to look for grass-fed milk, cheese, yogurt, and other dairy products whenever possible. If that is not possible, or if your budget does not allow for it, then aim for a lower percentage of fat (less than 2 percent), since the fat content in non-grass-fed dairy tends to have fewer nutrients. As far as non-dairy alternative milks, there are many options on the market now. If you have a milk allergy or lactose intolerance issue, it will probably be better for your overall well-being to pick an alternative; otherwise, dairy milk is OK. The recipes in this book were made with full-fat, grass-fed dairy but you can always substitute that for whatever you prefer. Just know that the nutritional content of the recipe may change (and that's OK!)

HOW TO PICK A NON-DAIRY ALTERNATIVE MILK?
Look at the ingredient list. Ideally you want one that has minimal ingredients and isn't loaded with sugar and/or flavorings. A few of my favorites include oat milk, soy milk, coconut milk, and almond milk. I tell most people, go based on ingredient labels and your taste buds, and you should be golden.

Plant-Based Meats/ Meat Alternatives

WHAT TO LOOK FOR:
Minimally-processed options

There are many plant-based "meats" on the market now, and many people assume they must be healthy since they include some plants. Sorry to break it to you, but many of these plant-based meat substitutes aren't very healthy, since they are more processed and full of additional ingredients. Certainly, if you choose to eat plant-based meat alternatives or prefer them, there is nothing wrong with that. Just know that it's not easy to regulate quality yet and that you'd be better off eating them occasionally than with every meal. (Impossible Foods makes plant-based meats that are among the better-quality products on the market.) Be sure to also consider other meat substitutes like tofu or tempeh, as these are far more natural and higher in quality than many of the overly-processed fake meat products.

Processed Food

WHAT TO LOOK FOR:
A short ingredient list

I'm not so naive to think that your whole grocery list will be void of processed foods. Mine isn't! So how do we know what to look for when shopping for processed foods? It really depends. If you are shopping for Halloween candy, just buy your favorites and move on with your life. If, however, you're buying a weekly staple like crackers, hummus, or bread, do your best to find a product with a shorter list of ingredients.

I understand the convenience of processed foods. That's why, even though we just discussed how quality food is an important part of a healthy diet, I don't expect that you'll never eat processed food. Instead, I want you to aim for some balance. I usually recommend my clients shoot for eating quality food and home-cooked meals 80 percent of the time, while letting the remaining 20 percent come in the form of processed food, takeout, and indulgences (hello, cupcakes!).

Far too often in my practice, I have found that if a client restricts themselves, they will eventually go down the path of bingeing. Instead of restricting yourself from eating processed foods like cookies, crackers, candy, and cakes, make them a smaller part of your life and even plan them into your weekly planner! Not sure how much to add in? It will depend on your goals and how you feel overall. Try adding in a dessert once or twice per week to see if that helps to satisfy a sweet craving, or add in a weekly pizza night once every other week. You're allowed to indulge occasionally, and you should be able to do it without feeling shameful or guilty. Just make it part of your plan!

WHAT IS QUANTITY?

When I talk about quantity, I'm talking about the amount of food you consume on your plate. This can take many different forms, but it often has to do with calories, macronutrients (a.k.a. "macros"), or portion size. In this planner, our goal is not to hyper-focus on how many calories and macros you need, but instead to give you some straightforward advice when it comes to quantity. After all, every day is different, so you shouldn't be dead set on a calorie goal. Instead, you should eat based on your hunger while making sure you are eating a balanced plate.

What Are Macros?

Macros are your macronutrients. These are components of food that are found in the largest quantity, unlike micronutrients (i.e., vitamins and minerals), which are found in much smaller quantities. They are necessary for the function of your body and overall health. There are three total macronutrients—carbohydrates, fats, and protein—and each is unique and important in its own right. Let's break them down so they are a bit easier to digest.

Carbohydrates

Carbohydrates, or "carbs," as many like to call them, provide energy for every system in your body. Carbs support intense exercise and even help to regulate blood sugar and insulin in the body. Your carbohydrate intake will affect all of your hormones and is necessary for the function of things like your thyroid. It's pretty powerful stuff.

WHERE TO FIND CARBS

- Fruits
- Vegetables

- Dairy

- Grains

- Legumes

- Refined/processed foods

HOW MANY CARBOHYDRATES DO YOU NEED?

This depends on your height, weight, age, sex, race, activity level, genetics, and more, but most people should aim to get 40 to 60 percent of their total daily intake from carbohydrates. Elite athletes may require more, especially during heavy training cycles. Each meal should contain some form of carbohydrate ranging from 30 to 60 grams or more, depending on your hunger and activity level. The average person needs a minimum of 150 grams of carbohydrates per day, though the exact number will vary from person to person.

WHAT DOES A SERVING OF CARBOHYDRATES LOOK LIKE?

One serving is about 15 grams of carbohydrates:

- 1 apple

- 1 slice of bread

- ½ cup sweet potato

- 1 cup milk

A NOTE ON FIBER

Fiber is an indigestible carbohydrate and is found in many carbohydrate-containing foods, like fruits, vegetables, and whole grains. Fiber keeps your bowels regulated, supports healthy blood sugar balance, and supports heart health. You will see fiber listed under each recipe in this planner. Aim for a goal of 25 to 40 grams per day.

Some examples of high-fiber foods:

- Apples

- Artichokes

- Avocado

- Beans

- Berries

- Broccoli

- Potatoes

- Nuts/seeds

- Oats

- Quinoa

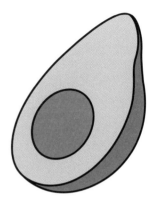

Protein

Protein is the building block of tissues in the body. It helps to maintain lean muscle mass and provide nourishment to parts of your body. It is essential to help you naturally detox your liver (you don't need a cleanse for that), and plays an important role in overall metabolism.

WHERE TO FIND PROTEIN

- Meat

- Poultry

- Eggs

- Seafood

- Nuts/seeds

- Soy

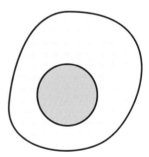

HOW MUCH PROTEIN DO YOU NEED?

Most people need 0.7 to 1 gram per pound of body weight, or 15 to 25 percent of their total daily intake. This usually means you need 20 to 30 grams of protein per meal and 10 to 20 grams of protein per snack, though the exact amount will vary based on a lot of different factors.

WHAT DOES A SERVING OF PROTEIN LOOK LIKE?

- 1 ounce of meat, poultry, or fish = 7 grams protein

- 1 egg = 6 to 7 grams protein

- 1 ounce nuts/seeds = 6 grams protein

- 2 tablespoons nut butter = 8 grams protein

- ½ cup cooked beans = 8 to 12 grams protein

- ½ cup tofu = 10 grams protein

Fat

Fat often gets a bad rep, but it is so incredibly powerful in the body. Fat helps to build hormones, modulate inflammation, and even keep us satisfied after a meal. Not only does fat make food taste good, but it also helps us absorb fat-soluble vitamins like A, D, E, and K. When we are purchasing fats, not all are created equal, so we do want to prioritize some fats over others. Healthy fats promote heart health, while unhealthy fats may lead to heart disease and/or inflammation. Some healthy fats include things like avocados, avocado oil, egg yolks, nuts, seeds, olive oil, and dark chocolate. Some fats that we may want to reduce our intake of (because they may lead to heart disease or inflammation) include trans fats; vegetable oils (like canola oil); saturated fats (like fat from conventionally-raised animals); full-fat dairy (especially if it is not grass-fed); and coconut oil. Try to limit your intake of the unhealthy fats and prioritize healthy fats whenever possible.

WHERE TO FIND HEALTHY FATS

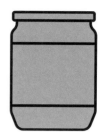

- Nuts/seeds

- Oils

- Butter

- Olives

- Avocado

HOW MUCH FAT DO YOU NEED?

Between 25 and 35 percent of your daily intake, or 60 to 100 grams per day. Less than 10% of your daily intake should come from saturated fat as well.

WHAT DOES A SERVING OF FAT LOOK LIKE?

- 1 teaspoon oil or butter

- 1 to 2 tablespoons salad dressing

- 1 to 2 tablespoons mayonnaise

- 1 to 2 tablespoons nut or seed butter

- 10 to 30 nuts, depending on type

- 10 olives

- ⅓ avocado

Putting it all together

Now that we've discussed what macros are and what serving sizes look like, it's time to put it all together. Short of giving you a direct prescription for how much you need daily (that is what seeing a dietitian is good for!), on the next page I've included some ways to assess portion sizes and build a meal. When you are putting together your portion sizes and plates, remember that no two people are alike, nor are any two days the same. We must keep in mind that variation in our portion sizes is normal and that listening to our hunger cues can be super helpful to help us dictate how much food we truly need.

HOW TO BUILD A BALANCED PLATE

Sometimes when it comes to portion size, it can be easier to visualize what should be on our plate. This illustration is a reference I use with my clients to help them understand how to build their plates for better health and improved overall satiety after a meal. While this reflects a person's normal dinner plate, it can certainly be used for any meal of the day.

Here is what you should aim to put on your plate for the other meals of the day.

BREAKFAST AND LUNCH

1 to 2 servings of carbohydrate (in the form of grains like oats, fruit like banana, dairy, or even vegetables)
20 to 30 grams of protein (in the form of eggs, protein powder, nuts/seeds, etc.)

SNACK

A snack should ideally have two of the three macronutrients (carb + fat, or protein + carb, or protein + fat). Portion sizes will depend on hunger. Refer to the list on page 15 and the recipes on page 84 for examples of ideal snacks.

HAND PORTION SIZE CHEAT SHEET

I find that while we don't need to count calories or macronutrients to be healthy, we may need to evaluate our portion sizes to ensure we are eating a healthy amount of food. Use this guide as a way to gauge if your serving sizes for certain foods make sense. It really can be this simple, so don't overthink it! This is not something that is set in stone but is a great starting point when you are building your meals.

Protein
One palmful

Dry Cereal
One fist

Raw Vegetables
Two fists

Rice/Noodles
One palmful

Cooked Vegetables
One fist

Slice of Bread
One full hand

Fruit
One fist

Nut Butters
One thumb

Dairy
One fist

Nuts/Seeds
One palmful

Cheese
One finger

Now that we've gone over both the importance of quality and quantity, it's time for you to start evaluating what is best for you to focus on first. Are you pretty good with quality? Great, work on ensuring you have a balanced plate at most meals. Feel like your quantity is great, but your quality is lagging behind? Now is the time to start focusing on ways to include quality foods into your routine (check out all the recipes following for inspiration). There is no one right way to approach your diet. Instead, approach it from an angle that you feel is lacking. Using the above guides and visuals can help you when planning out your week. The recipes in this book are a great place to start as they include a balanced approach to food and include plenty of protein, fiber and satisfying nutrients.

Suggested Kitchen Tools

Now that you are committed to the meal-planning life, you are going to want to ensure that you have the correct tools in your kitchen to be able to make yourself food week after week. It's easy to get swept up in the trends and think that you need every last gadget out there, but the good news is that you do not. This list is meant to show you the basics that will help you be successful in the kitchen. As you get more comfortable with meal prep and cooking, you may find other tools and gadgets that work well for you, but for now here are my top recommendations:

Sharp Chef's Knife and Cutting Board

These will help make the prep process more enjoyable because if you have to cut and prep items like vegetables, you want it to be easy. To keep the knife sharp, stock your kitchen with a sharpener, or visit your local kitchen store a few times per year—many do it free of charge. I recommend getting a large cutting board that can be used for small or large quantities of food; wood or plastic is fine. A large cutting board can help when you are making food ahead of time and getting all your food chopped without having to switch boards, unless it's raw meat, please switch boards for that.

Blender or Food Processor

You do not need both to be successful in the kitchen as they more or less do the same thing: pulverize food. That being said, if you want more shredding capability you may want to opt for the food processor. Having one of these on hand can shorten your meal prep time, which means that dinner is on the table sooner—who doesn't want that?

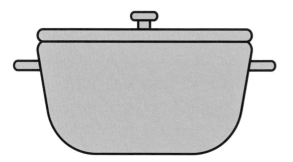

Slow Cooker or Pressure Cooker

While you can certainly have both, you really only need one of these options, as you can easily change a slow cooker recipe to be made in a pressure cooker and vice versa. In general, the pressure cooker will take less time to prepare the same meal as the slow cooker. Having a slow or pressure cooker for meal prep is essential, as you can cook big batches of food all at once with little cleanup.

Big Cast Iron Skillet

I love a cast iron skillet because it is so versatile, a large one can fit a lot of food, and it can go both on top of the stove and in the oven. It is also a great source of iron should you need an extra source in your diet. Having a large skillet means that meal prep for 1 or for 10 is manageable, so I always suggest a large one in case you want to double up on your recipes.

Large Dutch Oven or Pot

When making soups, stews, or one-pot pastas, having a reliable pot is as must. You can certainly invest in a set, but I often find I use my one enamel-coated Dutch oven for everything, as it cleans so easily, and one smaller stainless-steel pot to make rice or hard-boiled eggs. I recommend either enamel-coated cast iron or stainless steel, as nonstick pans raise some health and safety concerns because particles can come off while cooking. Having a large Dutch oven is essential for meal prepping soups, stews, or chilis on the weekend for the week ahead.

Sheet Pan(s)

If you want easy cleanup, sheet pans are where it's at. You can make an entire meal on one, making meal prep easy and cleaner, so don't skimp on size. The ones with sides are great for sheet-pan recipes, while the ones without are more for cookies, so pick the one (or both) that makes sense for what you need.

Storage Bags and Containers

Having the right storage containers can help with all the leftovers you make for the week. I prefer silicone storage bags because they are reusable, and glass containers because they clean easily. Start with a variety pack of each and then build from there, depending on the size of your family and how often you do your meal prep.

Can Opener

This may seem like a no-brainer, but there are a lot of meals that call for diced tomatoes or canned beans and you don't want to be hacking away at a can. Invest in a good can opener and it will last you for years to come and make meal prep that much easier.

Peeler

You can always use a knife to peel your fruits and veggies, but having a peeler does make it a little bit easier and less risky for your hands and fingers. And if you've noticed a theme, I prefer to make meal prep easier in any way I can.

Measuring Cups and Spoons

Sure, you can eyeball a few things here and there, but it is always helpful to have a set of cups, both wet (glass) and dry (metal), and a set of spoons to measure by teaspoons and tablespoons. Correct measuring ensures you can flavor your meals in the best way possible and get accurate results with your recipes.

Mixing Bowls

In my opinion, you can never have enough bowls in the kitchen. Start with small, medium, and large mixing bowls in glass or stainless steel, then add to your collection as you see fit. These are easy to wash and make it easy to mix anything, from salmon salad to protein bars.

Whisks and Spatulas

Unless you plan on mixing everything in the blender or by hand, a small and large whisk as well as a small and large spatula are helpful to mix and transfer food. Invest in a few because when some get dirty while meal prepping, it's nice to just grab a clean one and wash them all later.

Muffin Pan

If you want to make the egg cups on page 41, you're going to want a muffin tin. It's a necessity for meal prep and can be stored alongside your baking sheets.

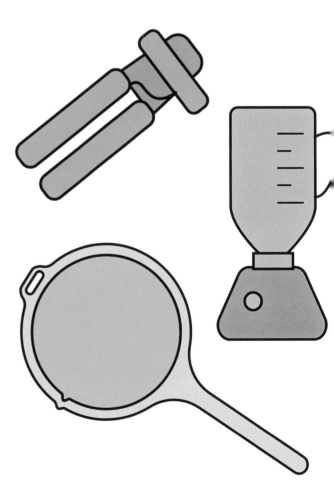

OTHER NICE-TO-HAVE KITCHEN TOOLS

The above items will get you started in the kitchen, but if you cook often, you may want other tools to help make your life even easier. Once you've stocked your kitchen with the above tools, think about treating yourself to some of these nice-to-have items to make the meal prep process easier and more enjoyable.

Immersion Blender

A handheld blender is especially great for those who have a small kitchen, as it takes up minimal space. You use it as you would a normal blender, but instead of putting contents into it, you bring the immersion blender to whatever bowl or pot you already have the food in. Great for quick blending of ingredients while meal prepping without a big mess.

Stand or Hand Mixer

While you can certainly mix most things by hand, it is nice to have the aid of a stand or hand mixer to make the process easier and faster. You don't need both, so pick whichever fits in your budget and your kitchen.

Silicone Mats and Cups

These are a great way to reduce overall waste in the kitchen, as you can reuse these mats and cups over and over and they wash pretty easily. The other great part is that you will never run out! Use these in place of aluminum foil or parchment paper in any of your recipes.

Thermometer

Cooking meat, poultry, and fish can be daunting to many, so instead of eyeballing it, grab a handheld thermometer to ensure your food is cooked through. (Check out www.foodsafety.gov for safe minimum cooking temperatures.) Now you know if your chicken is cooked to temperature and don't have to worry if you cooked it long enough or not.

Citrus Juicer

You can juice fruit by hand, but a citrus juicer will make the task easier and less messy. It also creates less waste, because you can get more juice out of each citrus fruit.

Bento Boxes

These partitioned stainless-steel or glass containers make for a fun lunch box idea. You will find a few recipes using these for lunch in this book, and while they're not necessary, they can definitely make meal prep more fun and interesting.

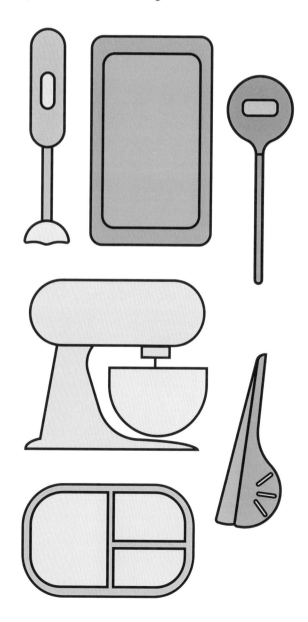

Breakfast Recipes

Make-ahead Freezer Burritos

30 MINUTES • SERVES 8

I like to work smarter, not harder, when it comes to breakfast. If it's not already prepared, I often find I push off eating or I just skip breakfast. These make-ahead burritos help to make breakfast a no-brainer: just grab one from the freezer and pop it in the microwave for 90 seconds and breakfast is served. Feel free to change up the veggies you use to make it different every time.

INGREDIENTS

1 pound ground breakfast sausage
2 large white potatoes, diced (about 1 ½ pounds)
1 bell pepper, diced
1 yellow onion, diced
8 large eggs
¼ cup milk of choice
1 ½ cups shredded cheddar cheese
½ teaspoon salt
¼ teaspoon black pepper
8 flour tortillas

NUTRITION FACTS (per serving)

Calories: 450
Carbs: 40g
Protein: 26g
Fat: 19g
Fiber: 5g

DIRECTIONS

1. Heat a large skillet over medium heat and add sausage. Cook until no longer pink, stirring occasionally.

2. Add potatoes and stir occasionally for 10 minutes, or until potatoes start to soften.

3. Add pepper and onion and cook for an additional 3 to 4 minutes, or until onion starts to turn translucent.

4. In a medium bowl, whisk eggs with milk, cheese, salt, and pepper.

5. Pour eggs over sausage and vegetable mixture and stir until eggs are cooked through.

6. Allow egg mixture to cool, then fill each tortilla with an equal portion of the egg mixture and roll to form a burrito. Enjoy immediately, or wrap each burrito individually in aluminum foil and/or parchment paper. Freeze wrapped burritos in a freezer-safe plastic bag for up to 2 months. Thaw overnight in refrigerator, then reheat in microwave for 60 seconds. If burrito is not thawed, reheat in microwave for 90 seconds or until heated through.

SWAPS

Gluten-Free

Use gluten-free tortillas

Dairy-Free

Use dairy-free milk and omit cheese or use dairy-free option

Vegan/Vegetarian

Use a meat alternative or tofu in place of the sausage; if vegan, use dairy-free milk, dairy-free cheese, and an "egg" substitute like scrambled tofu

Yogurt Parfaits

5 MINUTES • SERVES 2

Breakfast doesn't have to be hard, yet so often I see my clients overcomplicating it. A yogurt parfait breakfast keeps you full all morning, but doesn't require much prep work at all. You can buy granola or make your own; just look for one with less than 10 grams of added sugar per serving if at all possible.

INGREDIENTS

1 ⅓ cups plain Greek yogurt
½ cup granola
2 cups berries

NUTRITION FACTS (per serving)

Calories: 350
Carbs: 44g
Protein: 20g
Fat: 11g
Fiber: 8g

DIRECTIONS

1. In each of two 16-ounce glass containers, layer ⅓ cup yogurt, then 2 tablespoons granola, then ½ cup berries.

2. Repeat to layer the remaining ingredients in each container.

3. Enjoy immediately, or seal and store in the refrigerator for up to 2 days.

SWAPS

Gluten-Free
Look for granola that is gluten-free

Dairy-Free
Substitute dairy-alternative yogurt like almond or coconut

Vegan/Vegetarian
Recipe is already vegetarian. If vegan, substitute a dairy-free yogurt and make sure granola does not contain honey

Smoothie Bowl

5 MINUTES • SERVES 1

There is something more satisfying about a smoothie bowl than a smoothie. Maybe it's the fact that you can eat it more slowly with a spoon than you can with a straw. In any event, this recipe is super easy to make and customize, allowing for both simplicity and variety. I recommend portioning out your ingredients the night before and then combining them when you're ready to eat for the best consistency.

INGREDIENTS

1 cup frozen berries
1 banana
¼ cup milk of choice
1 tablespoon nut or seed butter
1 scoop protein powder

Toppings:
granola, chia seeds, sliced fruit, coconut flakes

NUTRITION FACTS (per serving)

Calories: 400
Carbs: 55g
Protein: 27g
Fat: 10g
Fiber: 10g

DIRECTIONS

1. Place frozen berries, banana, milk, nut or seed butter, and protein powder in a blender and blend on high for 60 seconds, or until smooth. Add water to thin if needed.

2. Pour into a medium bowl and top with your favorite toppings. Enjoy immediately.

SWAPS

Gluten-Free
Recipe is already gluten-free (choose gluten-free toppings)

Dairy-Free
Use dairy-free milk and plant-based protein powder

Vegan/Vegetarian
Recipe is already vegetarian. If vegan, use dairy-free milk and a plant-based protein powder

Apple Cinnamon Baked Oatmeal

35 MINUTES • SERVES 6

Oatmeal can get boring, but when you find different ways to make it, you can give this breakfast staple a fun makeover. This baked oatmeal is not only easy to prepare, it's also delicious. Feel free to change out the apples with whatever fruit is in season to make this dish relevant all year long.

INGREDIENTS

2 ½ cups rolled oats
1 teaspoon baking powder
1 teaspoon cinnamon
¼ teaspoon salt
2 large eggs
1 cup milk of choice
⅓ cup peanut butter
¼ cup maple syrup
1 teaspoon vanilla extract
2 small apples, chopped (1 ½ to 2 cups)

NUTRITION FACTS (per serving)

Calories: 326
Carbs: 46g
Protein: 11g
Fat: 12g
Fiber: 6g

DIRECTIONS

1. Preheat oven to 350°F and spray an 8x8-inch baking dish with cooking spray. Set aside.

2. In a large bowl, combine all ingredients except the apples until well mixed.

3. Fold in apples and spread mixture into the prepared baking dish.

4. Bake in oven for 30 to 40 minutes, or until center is baked through.

5. Allow to cool. Slice into 6 servings and enjoy immediately or store in refrigerator for up to 1 week.

SWAPS

Gluten-Free
Use certified gluten-free oats

Dairy-Free
Use dairy-free milk

Vegan/Vegetarian
Recipe is already vegetarian. If vegan, use dairy-free yogurt and milk and flax eggs (for each egg, mix 1 tablespoon flax meal with 2 ½ tablespoons water and let sit for 5 minutes)

Overnight Oats Five Ways

10 MINUTES PREP - 8 HOURS OVERNIGHT • SERVES 1

Overnight oats are one of my go-to breakfasts. They take less than five minutes to prep and you can make them the night before so they're ready to go. Feel free to up the protein content by adding some of your favorite protein powder.

BASE INGREDIENTS

½ cup rolled oats
½ cup milk of choice
1 teaspoon chia seeds
1 teaspoon maple syrup, or more to taste
½ teaspoon vanilla

DIRECTIONS

1. In a 2-cup glass container, combine all base ingredients and stir or shake to mix.

2. Add all ingredients for your variation of choice, then stir or shake to combine.

3. Seal container and place in the refrigerator for at least 8 hours. Enjoy within 3 days.

VARIATIONS

PB&J

½ cup berries
1 tablespoon peanut butter
1 tablespoon jelly

Lemon Blueberry

½ cup blueberries
1 tablespoon lemon curd
1 teaspoon lemon zest

Pumpkin Pie

2 tablespoons canned pumpkin
1 tablespoon pepitas
½ teaspoon cinnamon

Chocolate Peanut Butter Cup

1 tablespoon peanut butter
1 tablespoon chocolate chips
2 teaspoons cocoa powder

Cinnamon Roll

1 tablespoon raisins
1 tablespoon almond butter
½ teaspoon cinnamon

SWAPS

Gluten-Free
Use certified gluten-free oats

Dairy-Free
Use dairy-free milk

Vegan/Vegetarian
Recipe is already vegetarian. If vegan, use dairy-free milk

Overnight Oats Five Ways (cont.)

NUTRITION FACTS (per serving)

Base Recipe
Calories: 258
Carbs: 39g
Protein: 10g
Fat: 6g
Fiber: 5g

Pumpkin Pie
Calories: 309
Carbs: 44g
Protein: 12g
Fat: 10g
Fiber: 8g

PB&J
Calories: 446
Carbs: 67g
Protein: 14g
Fat: 15g
Fiber: 8g

Chocolate Peanut Butter Cup
Calories: 432
Carbs: 54g
Protein: 15g
Fat: 19g
Fiber: 8g

Lemon Blueberry
Calories: 369
Carbs: 61g
Protein: 11g
Fat: 9g
Fiber: 7g

Cinnamon Roll
Calories: 390
Carbs: 52g
Protein: 13g
Fat: 15g
Fiber: 8g

Egg Cups Five Ways

30 MINUTES • EACH VARIETY SERVES 6 (2 EGG CUPS PER SERVING)

Have you ever wanted eggs on a weekday morning but had no time to make them? That's where these egg cups come in! You can make a whole batch or two in the beginning of the week, then just grab them each morning, microwave really quickly, and you are on your way.

BASE INGREDIENTS

12 large eggs
⅓ cup milk of choice or water
½ teaspoon salt
Pinch of pepper

DIRECTIONS

1. Preheat oven to 350°F and grease a 12-cup muffin pan with cooking spray or butter.

2. In a large bowl, whisk together eggs, milk or water, and salt and pepper until frothy.

3. Divide all ingredients for your variation of choice evenly among the muffin cups, then pour egg mixture evenly over the top of each muffin cup.

4. Place in the oven and bake for 20 minutes, or until eggs are set and cooked through.

5. Remove and let cool. Store in an airtight container in the fridge and enjoy within a week. Alternatively, individually wrap egg muffins and store in the freezer for 1 to 2 months. Thaw overnight or reheat frozen in the microwave.

VARIATIONS

Broccoli, Bacon, and Cheddar

3 ½ cups chopped broccoli
6 slices bacon, cooked and crumbled
1 cup shredded cheddar cheese

Kale, Mushroom, and Swiss

2 cups torn kale leaves
2 cups chopped mushrooms
1 cup shredded Swiss cheese

Spinach, Tomato, and Feta

4 cups spinach
1 cup chopped cherry tomatoes
4 ounces feta, crumbled

Sausage, Pepper, and Onion

½ pound ground turkey sausage, cooked
1 bell pepper, chopped
½ yellow onion, chopped
1 cup shredded cheddar cheese

Mushroom, Pepper, and Spinach

4 cups spinach, chopped
1 cup chopped mushrooms
1 red bell pepper, chopped

Gluten-Free

Recipes are already gluten-free

Dairy-Free

Use water or dairy-free milk and omit cheese or use dairy-free option

Vegan/Vegetarian

Omit meat and stick to vegetable fillings. Vegan is not an option since there is no suitable egg replacement for this recipe

Egg Cups Five Ways (cont.)

NUTRITION FACTS (per serving)

Base Recipe

Calories: 150
Carbs: 1g
Protein:13g
Fat: 10g
Fiber: 0g

Spinach, Tomato, and Feta

Calories: 210
Carbs: 4g
Protein: 16g
Fat: 14g
Fiber: 1g

Broccoli, Bacon, and Cheddar

Calories: 355
Carbs: 6g
Protein: 23g
Fat: 27g
Fiber: 1g

Sausage, Pepper, and Onion

Calories: 294
Carbs: 4g
Protein: 25g
Fat: 19g
Fiber: 1g

Kale, Mushroom, and Swiss

Calories: 234
Carbs: 16g
Protein: 19g
Fat: 16g
Fiber: 1g

Mushroom, Pepper, and Spinach

Calories: 222
Carbs: 4g
Protein: 21g
Fat: 13g
Fiber: 1g

Protein Pancakes

20 MINUTES • SERVES 4

Who doesn't love pancakes for breakfast? I love making these ahead of time, then heating them up and topping them with yogurt, fruit, and maple syrup. These pancakes are filling but also a fun change for breakfast. The added yogurt contributes more protein and keeps you full longer, which is so important when it comes to breakfast.

INGREDIENTS

2 large eggs
1 cup plain Greek yogurt
½ cup milk of choice
2 tablespoons maple syrup
1 teaspoon vanilla
1 cup oat flour
2 teaspoons baking powder
½ teaspoon cinnamon
Pinch of salt

Optional mix-ins: blueberries, chocolate chips, chopped walnuts

NUTRITION FACTS (per serving)

Calories: 249
Carbs: 32g
Protein: 15g
Fat: 7g
Fiber: 3g

DIRECTIONS

1. In a large bowl, whisk together all ingredients.

2. Spray a large skillet with cooking spray and heat over medium heat.

3. Working in batches, add ¼ cup batter to skillet for each pancake and cook about 2 minutes, or until edges start to get dry and bubbles start to form. Flip pancakes and cook for an additional 1 to 2 minutes.

4. Repeat this process until all the batter is used up.

5. Enjoy immediately or store in an airtight container in the refrigerator for 3 to 4 days.

Gluten-Free
Use certified gluten-free oat flour

Dairy-Free
Use dairy-free yogurt and dairy-free milk

Vegan/Vegetarian
Recipe is already vegetarian. If vegan, use dairy-free yogurt and milk and flax eggs (for each egg, mix 1 tablespoon flax meal with 2 ½ tablespoons water and let sit for 5 minutes)

Lunch Recipes

Salmon Salad Lettuce Wraps

5 MINUTES • SERVES 4

Many people (myself included) grew up on tuna fish salad as a lunch option. However, have you ever tried salmon salad? It is a much milder-tasting (and smelling) meal and allows for variety in your lunches. Don't have canned salmon on hand? Feel free to use canned tuna in place of it.

INGREDIENTS

2 (5- to 6-ounce) cans salmon, drained

1 apple, diced

2 stalks celery, diced

¼ cup diced onion

½ teaspoon salt

¼ teaspoon pepper

¼ cup mayo, plus more as needed

Juice of ½ lemon

4 large iceberg or romaine lettuce leaves

NUTRITION FACTS (per serving)

Calories: 258

Carbs: 8g

Protein: 23g

Fat: 15g

Fiber: 2g

DIRECTIONS

1. In a small bowl, mix all ingredients except the lettuce together until well combined. Add extra mayo as needed for a smoother consistency.

2. Divide salmon salad among lettuce leaves, wrap lettuce around salad, and enjoy immediately, or store salmon salad and lettuce separately in the refrigerator for up to 5 days in an airtight container.

SWAPS

Gluten-Free
Recipe is already gluten-free

Dairy-Free
Recipe is already dairy-free

Vegan/Vegetarian
If vegan, use a plant-based or vegan mayo and replace the salmon with 1 (15.5-ounce) can of chickpeas, drained and mashed

Taco Salad Bowls

20 MINUTES • SERVES 6

Who doesn't love a good taco salad? This meal is super easy to make, and you can change it up by swapping in any vegetable or meat of your choice (like ground turkey or ground chicken) to keep it fresh each week.

INGREDIENTS

2 teaspoons avocado oil
1 pound lean ground beef
1 tablespoon taco seasoning (page 104 or store-bought)
1 (15-ounce) can black beans, drained and rinsed
1 (14.5-ounce) can diced tomatoes
½ cup prepared salsa
½ cup plain Greek yogurt
4 cups shredded iceberg or romaine lettuce
1 avocado, diced
1 cup shredded cheddar cheese

Optional toppings:
tortilla chips, cilantro, sliced radishes, chopped green onions, lime wedges

NUTRITION FACTS (per serving)
Calories: 421
Carbs: 22g
Protein: 30g
Fat: 24g
Fiber: 8g

DIRECTIONS

1. Heat oil in a large skillet, over medium-high heat. Add ground beef and taco seasoning and stir until no pink is showing, about 5 minutes.

2. Add black beans and tomatoes and cook for an additional 2 to 3 minutes until heated through. Remove from the heat.

3. Meanwhile in a small bowl, mix salsa and yogurt together; set aside.

4. Divide lettuce among six bowls and top each with an equal portion of the beef mixture, followed by avocado and cheese. Top with yogurt salsa and your toppings of choice.

5. Enjoy immediately. If meal prepping, store ground beef mixture and salsa mixture in separate airtight containers for up to 5 days.

SWAPS

Gluten-Free
Recipe is already gluten-free

Dairy-Free
Omit cheese (or use dairy-free option) and use dairy-free yogurt (or omit yogurt and just use salsa as topping)

Vegan/Vegetarian
Use a plant-based meat alternative. If vegan, use dairy-free cheese and omit yogurt

Turkey Hummus Sandwich

5 MINUTES • SERVES 1

Many of my clients come to me thinking that sandwiches are "bad" for them. I don't see food in terms as black and white as that. I see a sandwich and I see convenience. I'd much rather you get a sandwich packed for lunch then nothing at all. This is one of my favorite easy and quick lunches that keeps me full and satisfied. And there's nothing "bad" about it.

INGREDIENTS

2 slices wheat or whole-grain bread
2 tablespoons hummus
4 ounces deli turkey meat
1 slice provolone cheese
2 leaves romaine lettuce
2 slices tomato

NUTRITION FACTS (per serving)

Calories: 438
Carbs: 32g
Protein: 25g
Fat: 24g
Fiber: 4g

DIRECTIONS

1. Lightly toast the bread, if desired.

2. Spread hummus onto both slices of bread. Layer turkey, cheese, lettuce, and tomato on one slice, then top with the other slice. Enjoy immediately or pack for lunch the same day.

SWAPS

Gluten-Free
Use gluten-free bread

Dairy-Free
Omit cheese or use dairy-free cheese

Vegan/Vegetarian
Use plant-based deli slices and if vegan, omit cheese or use dairy-free cheese

Sesame Tofu Quinoa Bowls

40 MINUTES • SERVES 4

Ever get bored of your lunches? I know I do. This is one of those meals that I throw into the mix when I'm bored, and I find it always hits the spot. Feel free to add in your protein of choice if you aren't a tofu fan, or use rice or even cauliflower rice instead of quinoa.

INGREDIENTS

⅓ cup soy sauce

2 tablespoons sesame oil

1 tablespoon maple syrup

1 tablespoon sesame seeds

¼ teaspoon salt

¼ teaspoon black pepper

Pinch of red pepper flakes

1 (14-ounce) package extra-firm tofu, cubed and pressed (see Note)

1 head broccoli, chopped

1 red onion, sliced

2 cups cooked quinoa

4 cups spinach

1 avocado, sliced

½ cup sliced almonds

NUTRITION FACTS (per serving)

Calories: 507

Carbs: 40g

Protein: 25g

Fat: 31g

Fiber: 12g

DIRECTIONS

1. Preheat oven to 425°F and line a large baking sheet with parchment paper.

2. In a large bowl, whisk together soy sauce, sesame oil, maple syrup, sesame seeds, salt, pepper, and red pepper flakes. Add tofu, broccoli, and red onion to bowl and stir to coat evenly.

3. Spread tofu mixture out on parchment paper and place in oven for 30 minutes, or until tofu and broccoli are slightly crispy.

4. Meanwhile, to assemble quinoa bowls, fill each of four bowls or meal-prep containers with ½ cup quinoa, 1 cup spinach, and ¼ avocado.

5. When tofu is done, remove from the oven and let cool for 5 minutes, then add one-quarter of tofu mixture to each quinoa bowl. Top each bowl or container with 2 tablespoons sliced almonds.

6. Enjoy immediately or store in the refrigerator for 3 to 4 days. You may want to wait to add the avocado until the day you are going to eat this bowl.

NOTE

To press tofu, line a baking sheet with a layer of paper towels. Place tofu on top and cover with another layer of paper towels. Set a heavy object (like a filled tea kettle or baking dish) on top of tofu to press. Let sit for 30 to 60 minutes.

SWAPS

Gluten-Free

Use tamari or coconut aminos instead of soy sauce

Dairy-Free

Recipe is already dairy-free

Vegan/Vegetarian

Recipe is already vegan

BYO Salad That Doesn't Suck

10 MINUTES • EACH VARIETY SERVES 1

I don't know how many times I've heard someone say they hate salads, only to find out that what they actually hate is boring salads. Here's a pro tip: Your salad doesn't have to suck. Instead, you can make salads delicious by adding some interesting tastes and textures that will keep you coming back for more. Try the three versions here, or swap in any of your favorite greens, veggies, proteins, toppings, and dressings to create a version all your own. This is also a great way to use up any leftovers you have in the refrigerator.

DIRECTIONS

1. Place greens in a large bowl or airtight storage container. Top with vegetables, proteins, and toppings of choice.

2. When ready to serve, add oil, vinegar, citrus juice, and/or salt and pepper (depending on recipe) and toss.

3. Enjoy immediately. If meal prepping, store salad in an airtight container for up to 2 days in the refrigerator and add oil, vinegar, or any other dressing when you are ready to eat.

Classic Salad

INGREDIENTS

2 cups chopped romaine lettuce
½ cup shredded carrots
½ cup chopped cherry tomatoes
½ cup sliced cucumber
1 ounce cheddar cheese, cubed
4 ounces cooked chicken, chopped
1 tablespoon dried cranberries
1 tablespoon sliced almonds
½ tablespoon olive oil
½ tablespoon red wine vinegar
Salt and pepper to taste

NUTRITION FACTS (per serving)

Calories: 484
Carbs: 23g
Protein: 45g
Fat: 25g
Fiber: 5g

Strawberry Goat Cheese Salad

INGREDIENTS

2 cups spinach
½ cup sliced strawberries
¼ cup sliced radishes
¼ cup sliced red onion
1 ounce crumbled goat cheese
4 ounces tofu, cubed
½ avocado, sliced
1 tablespoon chopped walnuts
½ tablespoon olive oil
½ tablespoon balsamic vinegar
Salt and pepper to taste

NUTRITION FACTS (per serving)

Calories: 499
Carbs: 26g
Protein: 21g
Fat: 39g
Fiber: 12g

Mexican Chopped Salad

INGREDIENTS

2 cups spring mix
½ cup chopped cherry tomatoes
½ cup chopped bell pepper
¼ cup cooked black beans
4 ounces cooked chicken, chopped
1 ounce shredded cheddar cheese
½ avocado, sliced
½ tablespoon lime juice
Salt and pepper to taste

Optional toppings:
hot sauce and tortilla chips

NUTRITION FACTS (per serving)

Calories: 536
Carbs: 27g
Protein: 48g
Fat: 28g
Fiber: 13g

SWAPS

Gluten-Free

All salads are gluten-free

Dairy-Free

Classic Salad:
Omit cheddar cheese or use dairy-free option

Strawberry Goat Cheese Salad:
Omit goat cheese or use dairy-free option

Mexican Chopped Salad:
Omit cheddar cheese or use dairy-free option

Vegan/Vegetarian

Classic Salad: Omit cheese (or use dairy-free option) and swap chicken with tofu or tempeh

Strawberry Goat Cheese Salad:
Omit goat cheese or use dairy-free option

Mexican Chopped Salad: Omit cheese (or use dairy-free option) and swap chicken with tofu or tempeh

Buffalo Chicken Salad Wraps

10 MINUTES • SERVES 4

I love a good buffalo chicken dip, but I often don't want something that dense during the week. This buffalo chicken wrap seems indulgent, but it also helps you feel energized during the middle of your day (or anytime, really). If you don't have any yogurt, you can always use avocado or mayo to make it just as creamy.

INGREDIENTS

2 cups chopped cooked chicken
¼ cup hot sauce
¼ cup plain Greek yogurt
2 celery stalks, diced
½ red onion, diced
4 medium flour tortilla wraps
1 cup cherry tomatoes, halved
1 cup shredded lettuce

NUTRITION FACTS (per serving)

Calories: 286
Carbs: 24g
Protein: 32g
Fat: 7g
Fiber: 5g

DIRECTIONS

1. In a large bowl, combine chicken, hot sauce, and Greek yogurt and stir until evenly mixed.

2. Fold in celery and red onion.

3. Divide chicken evenly among tortilla wraps and top with cherry tomatoes and shredded lettuce. Fold in the sides of each tortilla and wrap like a burrito.

4. Enjoy warm or cold. Assembled wraps can be stored in the refrigerator for up to 1 day, or store the chicken mixture, lettuce, tomatoes, and wraps separately for up to 5 days before enjoying.

SWAPS

Gluten-Free
Use gluten-free wraps

Dairy-Free
Use mayo or avocado in place of yogurt

Vegan/Vegetarian
Use tofu in place of chicken. If vegan, swap vegan mayo, avocado, or dairy-free yogurt in for the yogurt

Bento Lunch Boxes Four Ways

10 MINUTES • EACH VARIETY SERVES 1

Most of us grew up taking a lunch box with us to school that contained a variety of food options. When I'd get bored of something, I'd just swap in another item. This is your grown-up school lunch box. Feel free to change up your protein, snack, or vegetable option to keep these boxes fun and in season. You can use a dedicated bento box-style container (which has different compartments) or simply use regular storage containers for your different ingredients.

Hard-Boiled Eggs

INGREDIENTS

2 hard-boiled eggs (page 104)
⅓ cucumber, sliced
2 tablespoons hummus
2 clementines
¼ cup trail mix

DIRECTIONS

1. Place all ingredients in a container.

2. Enjoy the same day or store in the refrigerator for up to 48 hours.

NUTRITION FACTS (per serving)

Calories: 472
Carbs: 43g
Protein: 22g
Fat: 26g
Fiber: 5g

Turkey & Cheese

INGREDIENTS

3 slices deli turkey meat
3 slices Swiss cheese
3 slices romaine or iceberg lettuce
10 baby carrots
2 tablespoons ranch dressing
1 cup grapes
¼ cup almonds

DIRECTIONS

1. Wrap deli meat around cheese and lettuce.

2. Place deli meat wraps, carrots, dressing, grapes, and almonds in a container.

3. Enjoy the same day or store in the refrigerator for up to 48 hours.

NUTRITION FACTS (per serving)

Calories: 526
Carbs: 38g
Protein: 25g
Fat: 32g
Fiber: 7g

 SWAPS

Gluten-Free

Use a gluten-free wrap or replace the wrap with lettuce for Hummus Veggie Box

Dairy-Free

Omit cheese (or use dairy-free option) and use dairy-free ranch for Turkey and Cheese box. Use mayo instead of yogurt for Tuna Salad box

Tuna Salad

INGREDIENTS

1 (5-ounce) can tuna in water, drained
½ celery stalk, diced
¼ cup plain Greek yogurt
1 teaspoon Dijon mustard
Fresh squeeze of lemon juice
Salt and pepper, to taste
2 iceberg lettuce leaves
½ bell pepper, sliced
1 apple, sliced
1 tablespoon peanut butter

DIRECTIONS

1. Mix tuna, celery, yogurt, mustard, lemon juice, salt, and pepper in a medium bowl.

2. Place lettuce in a container and top with tuna salad. Add bell pepper slices, apple slices, and peanut butter to the box.

3. Enjoy the same day or store in the refrigerator for up to 48 hours.

NUTRITION FACTS (per serving)

Calories: 360
Carbs: 39g
Protein: 31g
Fat: 11g
Fiber: 7g

Hummus Veggie Wrap

INGREDIENTS

1 whole-wheat wrap
2 tablespoons hummus
¼ cucumber, sliced
¼ bell pepper, sliced
1 cup shredded lettuce
2 celery stalks, sliced into sticks
1 tablespoon peanut butter
½ cup berries
1 tablespoon chocolate chips

DIRECTIONS

1. Spread hummus onto wrap, then top with cucumber, bell pepper, and lettuce.

2. Wrap tightly and slice into thirds.

3. Spread peanut butter on celery sticks.

4. Place wraps, celery with peanut butter, berries, and chocolate chips in an airtight container.

5. Enjoy the same day or store in the refrigerator for up to 48 hours.

NUTRITION FACTS (per serving)

Calories: 456
Carbs: 53g
Protein: 13g
Fat: 23g
Fiber: 11g

SWAPS

Vegan/Vegetarian

Use plant-based deli meat and cheese slices and replace ranch dressing with hummus for Turkey and Cheese box. Omit eggs and replace with tofu in Hard-Boiled Eggs box. Swap in one 15-ounce can chickpeas (drained and mashed) and vegan mayo for the tuna and yogurt in Tuna Salad box.

Roasted Chickpea Gyros

5 MINUTES • SERVES 4

I love eating crunchy chickpeas as a snack, but I had the idea one day to add them to a sandwich, and hence this recipe was born. Changing up the protein you use in your meals, like swapping in chickpeas for the usual gyro meat here, is a great way to stretch your budget and also to experiment with new flavors. Don't be afraid to add something like chicken or tofu to this meal should you want it a bit heartier.

INGREDIENTS

4 pieces pita bread
2 cups Crispy Chickpeas (page 87)
½ red onion, diced
1 cucumber, diced
1 cup halved cherry tomatoes
1 cup plain Greek yogurt
½ cup crumbled feta cheese
Fresh lemon slices
Salt and pepper to taste

NUTRITION FACTS (per serving)
Calories: 453
Carbs: 68g
Protein: 23g
Fat: 12g
Fiber: 11g

DIRECTIONS

1. Toast pita bread in toaster oven.

2. Fill each pita with ½ cup chickpeas, then divide the red onion, cucumber, and cherry tomatoes evenly among the pitas.

3. Top each gyro with ¼ cup Greek yogurt and 2 tablespoons feta cheese. Top with fresh lemon slices and salt and pepper to taste.

4. Serve immediately. If preparing ahead, store chickpeas in an airtight container for up to 1 week in a dark, cool place. Store remaining toppings separately in airtight containers in the refrigerator for up to 5 days.

SWAPS

Gluten-Free
Use gluten-free pita or lettuce wraps

Dairy-Free
Use dairy-free yogurt and omit feta cheese (or use dairy-free option)

Vegan/Vegetarian
Recipe is already vegetarian. If vegan, use dairy-free yogurt and omit feta cheese (or use dairy-free option)

Pressure Cooker Lentil Tortilla Soup

30 MINUTES • SERVES 6

Sometimes you want a meal that is filling but not hard to make. This hearty recipe couldn't be easier: You just dump ingredients in a pot, set it, and forget it. It doesn't get simpler than that! If you want to use meat in this recipe, feel free to add your favorite ground meat, but the beans make this dish incredibly filling, so you may not even notice it's a meatless entrée. If you don't have a pressure cooker, you can also make this in a slow cooker; it will need at least 4 hours to cook.

INGREDIENTS

1 tablespoon avocado oil

3 cloves garlic, minced

1 yellow onion, diced

1 bell pepper, diced

1 jalapeño, seeded and diced

2 cups vegetable broth

2 (14.5-ounce) cans diced tomatoes

1 (15-ounce) can black beans

1 (15-ounce) can pinto beans

1 cup dried lentils

2 tablespoons taco seasoning (page 104 or store-bought)

1 tablespoon tomato paste

Optional toppings:
shredded cheddar cheese, jalapeño slices, tortilla chips

DIRECTIONS

1. Place avocado oil in the pressure cooker and set the cooker to sauté. Add garlic, onion, bell pepper, and jalapeño and sauté for 3 minutes.

2. Turn off the heat and add broth, tomatoes, black beans, pinto beans, lentils, taco seasoning, and tomato paste. Stir to combine.

3. Close the pressure cooker, lock lid, and pressure cook on high for 15 minutes.

4. Allow pressure to naturally release for 10 minutes, then manually release any remaining pressure.

5. Divide soup among six bowls and sprinkle with toppings of choice.

NUTRITION FACTS (per serving)

Calories: 457

Carbs: 86 g

Protein: 30g

Fat: 3g

Fiber: 22g

NOTE

To prepare in a slow cooker, place all ingredients in the slow cooker and stir to combine. Cook on high for 4 to 6 hours or on low for 6 to 8 hours, or until lentils are cooked through.

SWAPS

Gluten-Free
Recipe is already gluten-free

Dairy-Free
Recipe is already dairy-free

Vegan/Vegetarian
Recipe is already vegan

Dinner Recipes

Slow Cooker Chili

**15 MINUTES PREP • COOK TIME: 7-8 HOURS
SERVES 8**

There is nothing like the smell of your kitchen after chili has been cooking all day long. But chili is also one of my favorite meal-prep meals, because it takes minimal effort and it makes a lot of food. Even if you don't need it all right now, you can always freeze it and have it ready to pull out during a week where you're super busy.

INGREDIENTS

1 tablespoon avocado oil
2 pounds lean ground beef
1 yellow onion, chopped
1 bell pepper, chopped
1 jalapeño, seeded and sliced
3 cloves garlic, minced
2 cups beef broth
2 (15-ounce) cans black beans, drained
1 (28-ounce) can diced tomatoes
1 (6-ounce) can tomato paste
2 tablespoons chili powder
2 teaspoons paprika
2 teaspoons cumin
1 teaspoon oregano
1 teaspoon salt
½ teaspoon black pepper

NUTRITION FACTS (per serving)
Calories: 372
Carbs: 28g
Protein: 32g
Fat: 14g
Fiber: 10g

DIRECTIONS

1. Heat oil in large skillet, over medium heat. Add ground beef and cook, stirring occasionally until no pink is showing, about 6 to 7 minutes.

2. Add onion, bell pepper, jalapeño, and garlic and cook for 3 to 4 minutes, or until onion starts to soften.

3. Remove from the heat and transfer to the slow cooker. Add the rest of the ingredients to the slow cooker and stir to combine.

4. Cover and cook on low for 7 to 8 hours, or on high for 5 to 6 hours.

5. Serve immediately, store in an airtight container in the refrigerator for 1 week, or freeze individual servings in freezer-safe containers for up to 3 months.

SWAPS

Gluten-Free
Recipe is already gluten-free

Dairy-Free
Recipe is already dairy-free

Vegan/Vegetarian
Use a plant-based ground meat alternative, and use vegetable broth instead of beef broth

One-Skillet Chicken Fajitas

25 MINUTES • SERVES 4

You know what I love even more than an easy recipe? An easy cleanup. This one-skillet recipe offers both, so it's a win-win in my household. Having just one pan to clean means I can get to the best part more quickly: eating!

INGREDIENTS

1 ½ pounds chicken breast, sliced thin
2 tablespoons avocado oil, divided
1 teaspoon chili powder
1 teaspoon paprika
½ teaspoon cumin
½ teaspoon salt
¼ teaspoon black pepper
3 bell peppers, sliced thin
1 yellow onion, sliced thin
Juice of ½ lime
¼ cup chopped cilantro, optional
Rice or tortillas, for serving

NUTRITION FACTS (per serving)

Calories: 321
Carbs: 13g
Protein: 40g
Fat: 12g
Fiber: 3g

DIRECTIONS

1. In a large bowl, combine chicken, 1 tablespoon of oil, and spices; stir to mix.

2. In a large skillet, heat remaining 1 tablespoon of oil over medium heat. Add chicken to skillet and cook, stirring until no longer pink, 8 to 10 minutes.

3. Add peppers and onions and continue cooking for 5 minutes, until flavors are combined and peppers and onions begin to soften.

4. Remove from heat and top with lime juice and cilantro, if using.

5. Enjoy immediately over rice or in tortillas, or store in an airtight container in the refrigerator for up to 5 days.

SWAPS

Gluten-Free
Recipe is already gluten-free

Dairy-Free
Recipe is already dairy-free

Vegan/Vegetarian
Use sliced tofu instead of chicken breast

Mongolian Beef Ramen

25 MINUTES • SERVES 4

I used to think ramen was just the square package with a very salty packet included. I didn't realize how versatile it could be in meal prep. Not only is it tasty, but it cooks so fast (faster than pasta) that it makes for a simple carb to add to your meal. Enjoy it with one of my favorite beef-and-broccoli combinations in this one-skillet Mongolian beef dish.

INGREDIENTS

1 tablespoon avocado oil
1 pound flank steak, sliced thin against the grain
2 tablespoons cornstarch
2 small heads broccoli, chopped
1 carrot, sliced into matchsticks
10 ounces ramen noodles, uncooked
4 whole green onions, chopped
Sesame seeds, for garnish

SAUCE

1 cup chicken broth
½ cup soy sauce
1 tablespoon sesame oil
3 cloves garlic, minced
1 tablespoon brown sugar
Pinch of red pepper flakes

NUTRITION FACTS (per serving)

Calories: 581
Carbs: 72g
Protein: 37g
Fat: 18g
Fiber: 5g

DIRECTIONS

1. In a large skillet, heat avocado oil over medium heat. Meanwhile, in a medium bowl, toss steak with cornstarch to evenly coat.

2. Add steak to skillet and cook until browned on both sides, about 3 minutes per side. Remove steak from skillet and set aside.

3. In the same skillet, combine all ingredients for the sauce and whisk together . Add broccoli and carrots, reduce heat to medium-low, cover, and cook until vegetables are tender, about 5 minutes.

4. Remove cover and return steak to the skillet, then add ramen noodles. Stir noodles and break them up as they start to soften, cooking for another 2 to 3 minutes to allow some of the broth to evaporate.

5. Divide among bowls, top with green onions and sesame seeds, and enjoy immediately, or store in an airtight container in the refrigerator for 4 to 5 days.

Gluten-Free

Use gluten-free ramen noodles or rice noodles, and use tamari or coconut aminos instead of soy sauce

Dairy-Free

Recipe is already dairy-free

Vegan/Vegetarian

Use vegetable broth instead of chicken broth. Use sliced tofu or plant-based meat alternative in place of beef

Turkey Stuffed Peppers

30 MINUTES • SERVES 4 (2 half peppers per serving)

I love stuffed peppers because they're an easy way to get vegetables on the plate. For whatever reason, eating the pepper as a shell makes it more fun for everyone. If someone isn't into the whole pepper, feel free to chop it up after cooking.

INGREDIENTS

1 tablespoon avocado oil
1 pound ground turkey
1 yellow onion, diced
3 cloves garlic, minced
1 jalapeño, seeded and diced
1 (14.5-ounce) can diced tomatoes
2 teaspoons chili powder
1 teaspoon cumin
½ teaspoon salt
¼ teaspoon black pepper
1 ½ cups cooked white rice
4 bell peppers, seeded and sliced in half
1 cup shredded cheddar cheese

NUTRITION FACTS (per serving)

Calories: 502
Carbs: 29g
Protein: 35g
Fat: 28g
Fiber: 5g

DIRECTIONS

1. Preheat oven to 400°F.

2. Heat oil in a large skillet over medium heat. Add ground turkey and cook, stirring until no longer pink, about 6 to 7 minutes.

3. Add onions and garlic and cook for 3 minutes, or until onion is translucent. Add jalapeño and cook for 1 minute more.

4. Add diced tomatoes and spices and stir to combine, then remove from the heat and stir in rice.

5. Place bell peppers sliced side up on a large, greased baking dish. Fill each pepper half with meat and rice mixture. Top with cheese and bake uncovered for 20 minutes.

6. Enjoy immediately, store in an airtight container for up to 5 days in the refrigerator, or freeze individual servings in freezer-safe containers for up to 3 months.

SWAPS

Gluten-Free

Recipe is already gluten-free

Dairy-Free

Omit cheese or use dairy-free option

Vegan/Vegetarian

Use a plant-based ground meat alternative and if vegan, omit cheese or use dairy-free option

Greek Chicken Bowls

30 MINUTES • SERVES 4

Do you have a set of skewers gathering dust in the back of a drawer? Let this recipe be a reminder to take them out and use them. Skewers allow you to cook a lot of meat in a shorter amount of time, which makes these Greek chicken bowls great for meal prepping or even to make as a last-minute meal.

INGREDIENTS

1 ½ pounds chicken breast, cubed
¼ cup olive oil
Juice of 1 lemon
3 cloves garlic, minced
1 tablespoon oregano
½ teaspoon salt
¼ teaspoon black pepper
Pinch of red pepper flakes, optional
2 red bell peppers, cut into 1-inch pieces
1 red onion, coarsely chopped
4 cups arugula
2 cups cooked white rice
½ cup hummus
¼ cup crumbled feta cheese
1 cucumber, diced
Optional toppings: sliced cherry tomatoes, pita bread, kalamata olives

NUTRITION FACTS (per serving)

Calories: 524
Carbs: 33g
Protein: 44g
Fat: 24g
Fiber: 5g

DIRECTIONS

1. In a medium bowl, combine chicken with oil, lemon juice, garlic, oregano, salt, pepper, and red pepper flakes, if using. Stir to coat evenly. Cover and let marinate in the refrigerator for 20 minutes or up to 2 hours.

2. Preheat oven or grill to 450°F. If using oven, line a large baking sheet with aluminum foil and set aside.

3. Thread chicken, red bell pepper, and red onion onto skewers. To grill, place on grill and cook for 5 to 7 minutes per side, or until chicken's internal temperature is 165°F. If using oven, place skewers on the prepared baking sheet and bake for 20 to 25 minutes, or until chicken reaches an internal temperature of 165°.

4. When ready to assemble, place 1 cup arugula and ½ cup rice in each bowl. Remove chicken and vegetables from the skewers and divide evenly among the bowls, then top with hummus, feta, and diced cucumber. Add your toppings of choice.

5. Enjoy immediately, or store chicken skewers and other bowl ingredients separately for up to 5 days in the refrigerator and assemble when ready to eat.

SWAPS

Gluten-Free

Recipe is already gluten-free

Dairy-Free

Omit feta cheese or use dairy-free option

Vegan/Vegetarian

Use tofu in place of chicken and if vegan, omit feta cheese or use dairy-free option

Sheet Pan Teryiaki Chicken & Veggies

35 MINUTES • SERVES 4

As I said earlier, sheet pan recipes are some of my favorite recipes because they are both easy to make and easy to clean up. I find many of us get overwhelmed not only by preparing dinner, but also the cleaning up that comes with it. This one is super easy, and you don't have to stress about dishes galore once you're done.

INGREDIENTS

1 ½ pounds chicken breast, sliced
1 large head broccoli, chopped
1 red bell pepper, sliced
2 large carrots, cut into matchsticks
2 cups sugar snap peas

TERYIAKI SAUCE

⅓ cup soy sauce
2 tablespoons honey
1 tablespoon sesame oil
2 teaspoons sesame seeds
1 teaspoon fresh grated ginger
2 cloves garlic, minced
¼ teaspoon black pepper

NUTRITION FACTS (per serving)
Calories: 351
Carbs: 24g
Protein: 45g
Fat: 9g
Fiber: 5g

DIRECTIONS

1. Preheat oven to 400°F and line a baking sheet with aluminum foil or parchment paper.

2. In a large bowl, whisk together all ingredients for teriyaki sauce. Add chicken and veggies and stir to coat evenly.

3. Spread mixture out on the baking sheet in one even layer and place in oven. Bake for 25 to 30 minutes, or until chicken reaches an internal temperature of 165°F.

4. Enjoy immediately by itself or over rice, or store in an airtight container in the refrigerator for up to 5 days.

SWAPS

Gluten-Free
Use tamari or coconut aminos instead of soy sauce

Dairy-Free
Recipe is already dairy-free

Vegan/Vegetarian
Swap chicken for tofu. If vegan, use brown sugar instead of honey

One-Pot Taco Pasta

30 MINUTES • SERVES 6

As if tacos weren't easy enough, this one-pot taco pasta is even easier. I love any rendition of the taco because it's a flavor profile that almost everyone in the family can get behind. This one-pot taco pasta will be your family's new go-to weeknight dinner.

INGREDIENTS

1 tablespoon olive oil

1 yellow onion, diced

1 red bell pepper, diced

3 cloves garlic, minced

1 pound ground turkey

1 (15-ounce) can black beans

1 (14.5-ounce) can diced tomatoes

1 tablespoon taco seasoning (page 104 or store-bought)

3 cups water or broth

8 ounces chickpea pasta shells

1 ½ cups cheddar cheese

Optional toppings: cilantro, jalapeño slices, sliced tomatoes, sour cream

NUTRITION FACTS (per serving)

Calories: 551

Carbs: 41g

Protein: 40g

Fat: 27g

Fiber: 11g

DIRECTIONS

1. Heat oil in a large pot over medium heat.

2. Add onion, pepper, and garlic and cook, stirring, for 3 minutes, or until onion starts to soften.

3. Add ground turkey and cook, stirring until no longer pink, 5 to 7 minutes.

4. Add black beans, diced tomatoes, and taco seasoning and stir to combine.

5. Add water or broth and bring to a slow boil.

6. Add pasta and cook, stirring frequently, for 8 to 10 minutes, or until pasta is done.

7. Stir in cheese.

8. Enjoy immediately with your toppings of choice or store in an airtight container in the refrigerator for up to 1 week.

SWAPS

Gluten-Free

Make sure chickpea pasta is gluten-free

Dairy-Free

Omit cheese or use dairy-free option

Vegan/Vegetarian

Use plant-based meat alternative in place of the turkey. If vegan, omit cheese or use dairy-free option

Spaghetti Squash & Meatballs

45 MINUTES • SERVES 4

I grew up in an Italian household, so pasta and meatballs were a Sunday staple. However, I wanted to add a bit more nutritional value to the old classic. Spaghetti squash is easy to make and has more vitamins and minerals than pasta. That being said, if you are short on time or can't find spaghetti squash, feel free to use your favorite pasta.

INGREDIENTS

1 medium spaghetti squash, cut in half lengthwise and seeds scooped out
½ teaspoon salt
¼ teaspoon black pepper
1 pound lean ground beef
1 large egg
¼ cup grated Parmesan cheese, plus more for topping
1 clove garlic, minced
2 teaspoons parsley, plus more for topping
2 teaspoons oregano
½ teaspoon salt
¼ teaspoon black pepper
Marinara sauce (page 107 or store-bought)

NUTRITION FACTS (per serving)

Calories: 383
Carbs: 26g
Protein: 30g
Fat: 18g
Fiber: 5g

DIRECTIONS

1. Preheat oven to 400°F. Line two large baking sheets with aluminum foil.

2. Sprinkle cut sides of spaghetti squash with salt and pepper. Place both halves cut side down on one baking sheet. Bake in the oven for 40 minutes, or until squash pulls easily away from skin.

3. Meanwhile, in a large bowl, mix all ingredients for meatballs until evenly combined. Form into golf ball-sized meatballs and place on the second baking sheet. Transfer to the oven and bake for 20 minutes.

4. While waiting for the squash and meatballs, heat marinara sauce in saucepan on low.

5. When meatballs are done, add meatballs to marinara sauce and allow flavors to meld for about 10 minutes over low heat, until spaghetti squash is done.

6. To serve, use two forks to pull the spaghetti squash apart into strands and divide among four plates, then top with the meatballs and sauce. Serve with Parmesan cheese and parsley flakes. Store leftovers in an airtight container in the refrigerator for up to 5 days.

SWAPS

Gluten-Free

Recipe is already gluten-free

Dairy-Free

Replace Parmesan cheese with breadcrumbs or almond meal

Vegan/Vegetarian

Use ground plant-based meat alternative. If vegan, replace Parmesan cheese with breadcrumbs or almond meal

Tacos Five Ways

15-40 MINUTES • EACH VARIETY SERVES 4

Tacos are a go-to in my household. Often my clients say they love tacos, but they don't think they are a healthy option. I'm going to challenge that thinking, because with the right ingredients, they're not only a healthy option, but also a very convenient and delicious option. I've included five of my favorite taco varieties to make Taco Tuesday (or any day of the week) easy and fun for the whole family.

Carne Asada (Beef)

INGREDIENTS

Juice of 2 limes
½ cup orange juice
2 tablespoons avocado oil
2 tablespoons apple cider vinegar
½ cup chopped cilantro
1 jalapeño, minced
3 cloves garlic, minced
1 teaspoon onion powder
½ teaspoon cumin
½ teaspoon salt
¼ teaspoon black pepper
1 ½ pounds flank steak
8 tortillas of choice

Optional toppings: chopped onion, pico de gallo, crumbled cotija cheese, sliced jalapeños, chopped avocado

NUTRITION FACTS (filling only, per serving)
Calories: 372
Carbs: 7g
Protein: 37g
Fat: 21g
Fiber: 1g

DIRECTIONS

1. In a medium bowl, whisk together lime juice, orange juice, avocado oil, apple cider vinegar, cilantro, jalapeño, garlic, and spices to form a marinade.

2. Place steak and marinade in a large plastic bag and marinate in the refrigerator for 20 minutes or overnight.

3. Preheat grill to medium-high heat. Remove steak from marinade, letting any excess drip off, and grill to desired doneness, 5 to 6 minutes per side for medium doneness.

4. Slice or cube steak and enjoy immediately in your favorite tortillas with your favorite toppings, or store steak in an airtight container in the refrigerator for up to 5 days.

Tacos Five Ways (cont.)

Shrimp and Cilantro Slaw

INGREDIENTS

1 (14-ounce) bag coleslaw mix

¼ cup cilantro

1 jalapeño, seeded and minced

1 cup plain Greek yogurt

Juice of 2 limes

2 tablespoons avocado oil, divided

½ teaspoon cumin

Pinch of salt

Pinch of black pepper

1 pound Shrimp, peeled and deveined

1 tablespoon taco seasoning (page 104 or store-bought)

8 tortillas of choice

NUTRITION FACTS (filling only, per serving)

Calories: 223

Carbs: 16g

Protein: 30g

Fat: 5g

Fiber: 4g

DIRECTIONS

1. In a medium bowl, combine coleslaw mix, cilantro, jalapeño, Greek yogurt, lime juice, 1 tablespoon of oil, the cumin, salt, and pepper and stir to mix. Cover and refrigerate until ready to use.

2. In a large skillet, heat remaining 1 tablespoon oil over medium heat. Add shrimp and taco seasoning and cook 2 to 3 minutes per side.

3. To enjoy immediately, serve shrimp in your favorite tortillas topped with cilantro slaw, or store shrimp and slaw in separate airtight containers in the refrigerator for 2 to 3 days.

SWAPS

Gluten-Free

Use corn tortillas

Dairy-Free

Recipes are already dairy-free

Vegan/Vegetarian

Stick to the veggie tacos

Mushroom and Veggie Tacos

INGREDIENTS

1 tablespoon avocado oil

1 red onion, sliced thin

1 red bell pepper, sliced thin

4 portobello mushroom caps, sliced

1 tablespoon taco seasoning (page 104 or store-bought)

8 tortillas of choice

Optional toppings: pico de gallo, guacamole, crumbled cotija cheese, sliced jalapeños

NUTRITION FACTS (filling only, per serving)

Calories: 97

Carbs: 12g

Protein: 5g

Fat: 5g

Fiber: 4g

DIRECTIONS

1. Heat oil in a large skillet over medium heat.

2. Add onion and pepper and cook, stirring, for 3 to 4 minutes, or until onion starts to turn translucent.

3. Add mushrooms and taco seasoning and cook for 5 minutes, stirring until mushrooms start to reduce in size.

4. Enjoy immediately in your favorite tortillas with your favorite toppings, or store veggies in an airtight container in the refrigerator for up to 5 days.

Shredded Chicken

INGREDIENTS

1 ½ pounds chicken breast

1 tablespoon avocado oil

1 (14.5-ounce) can diced tomatoes

2 tablespoons tomato paste

1 tablespoon taco seasoning (page 104 or store-bought)

8 tortillas of choice

NUTRITION FACTS (filling only, per serving)

Calories: 262

Carbs: 5g

Protein: 39g

Fat: 8g

Fiber: 1g

DIRECTIONS

1. Bring a large pot of water to boil. Add chicken and boil for 10 to 20 minutes, or until cooked through to an internal temperature of 165°F.

2. Let chicken cool, then use two forks or a stand mixer to shred chicken.

3. Heat oil in a medium skillet over medium heat, then add shredded chicken, tomatoes, tomato paste, and taco seasoning. Stir to combine, then cook for 5 minutes.

4. To enjoy immediately, serve chicken in your favorite tortillas with your favorite toppings, or store chicken in an airtight container in the refrigerator for up to 5 days.

Tacos Five Ways (cont.)

Ground Turkey

INGREDIENTS

1 tablespoon avocado oil

1 yellow onion, diced

2 cloves garlic, minced

1 pound ground turkey

2 tablespoons tomato paste

2 tablespoons taco seasoning (page 104 or store-bought)

8 tortillas of choice

Optional toppings: lettuce, tomato, avocado, shredded cheese, sliced olives, and sour cream

NUTRITION FACTS (filling only, per serving)

Calories: 221

Carbs: 5g

Protein: 22g

Fat: 13g

Fiber: 1g

DIRECTIONS

1. Heat oil in a large skillet over medium heat.

2. Add onion and garlic and cook, stirring, for 3 to 4 minutes, or until onion starts to turn translucent.

3. Add ground turkey, tomato paste, and taco seasoning. Cook, stirring for about 6 to 7 minutes until turkey is cooked through and no longer pink.

4. Serve immediately in your favorite tortillas with your favorite toppings, or store turkey in an airtight container in the refrigerator for up to 5 days.

Shrimp Stir-Fry

20 MINUTES • SERVES 4

Shrimp is one of the easiest proteins to cook in a hurry, so I keep a 2-pound bag in my freezer at all times. When I need a quick dinner, I throw the shrimp in a bowl of ice-cold water and it's thawed in no time at all. This recipe is a favorite last-minute way to get dinner on the table, as I almost always have these ingredients at home—and if I don't, it's easy to swap in whatever veggies I do have on hand and throw it over some rice for a complete meal.

INGREDIENTS

½ cup vegetable broth
3 tablespoons soy sauce
1 teaspoon honey
1 teaspoon cornstarch
2 tablespoons sesame oil, divided
3 cloves garlic, minced
1 pound shrimp, peeled and deveined
½ teaspoon salt, plus more to taste
¼ teaspoon black pepper, plus more to taste
1 large head broccoli, chopped
2 cups snow peas
1 red bell pepper, sliced
5 green onions, trimmed and sliced
Cooked rice or cauliflower rice, optional

NUTRITION FACTS (per serving)

Calories: 228
Carbs: 14g
Protein: 28g
Fat: 8g
Fiber: 4g

DIRECTIONS

1. In a small bowl, whisk together broth, soy sauce, honey, and cornstarch; set aside.

2. In a large skillet, heat 1 tablespoon of sesame oil over medium heat. Add garlic and cook for 1 minute.

3. Add shrimp and cook for 2 to 3 minutes per side, or until pink and no longer translucent. Season with salt and pepper, then remove shrimp from skillet and set aside.

4. Add remaining 1 tablespoon of sesame oil to skillet and add broccoli, snow peas, red pepper, and green onions. Cook, stirring for 3 to 4 minutes, or until pepper starts to soften.

5. Pour in broth mixture and toss to coat, then add shrimp back in and cook until heated through, about 2 minutes. Add additional salt and pepper to taste.

6. Serve on its own or over rice or cauliflower rice, or store in an airtight container in the refrigerator for up to 2 days.

SWAPS

Gluten-Free
Use tamari or coconut aminos instead of soy sauce

Dairy-Free
Recipe is already dairy-free

Vegan/Vegetarian
Use tofu instead of shrimp (cooking time will change, as tofu may take about 6-8 minutes to heat through). If vegan, use brown sugar in place of honey

Build Your Own Burrito Bowl

15 MINUTES • SERVES 4

You can always go to your local fast-casual burrito spot, but wouldn't it be easier on your budget if you could make a great burrito bowl at home? Definitely. Learning how simple it can be to make your own burrito bowl is empowering. Swap in whatever ingredients you are in the mood for, or make use of leftovers before they go bad.

INGREDIENTS

1 tablespoon olive oil
1 green bell pepper, sliced
1 small red onion, sliced
2 cups cooked rice
4 cups shredded romaine lettuce
½ cup salsa
1 (15-ounce) can black beans, drained
1 pound cooked chicken (Easy Baked Chicken or Simple Ground Meat, page 105), cooked with 1 to 2 teaspoons taco seasoning (page 104 or store-bought) instead of salt and pepper
2 avocados, chopped
½ cup shredded cheddar cheese

Optional toppings: plain Greek yogurt or sour cream, sliced jalapeños

NUTRITION FACTS (per serving)

Calories: 662
Carbs: 53g
Protein: 51g
Fat: 29g
Fiber: 16g

DIRECTIONS

1. Heat oil in a medium skillet over medium-high heat. Add peppers and onions and cook, stirring frequently, for 5 minutes, until peppers begin to blister and onions soften. Remove from the heat.

2. To assemble the burrito bowls, place ½ cup rice, 1 cup shredded lettuce, and 2 tablespoons salsa in each bowl. Add one-quarter of the black beans, meat, and avocado to each bowl, then top each serving with 2 tablespoons cheese. Serve immediately with your toppings of choice. If meal prepping, store all ingredients separately until ready to eat and then assemble day-of.

Gluten-Free
Recipe is already gluten-free

Dairy-Free
Omit cheddar cheese or use dairy-free option

Vegan/Vegetarian
Use cubed tofu or ground plant-based meat alternative in place of chicken. If vegan, omit cheddar cheese or use dairy-free option

Snacks

Homemade Trail Mix

5 MINUTES • SERVES 8

Trail mix is an easy and filling snack you can make for the whole family to enjoy. I often find the ones at the store are loaded with sugar and have very few servings in the bag or container, which means they're not the best value. Make this in a big batch for the week, and feel free to swap in different nuts, seeds, and dried fruit based on what you have on hand. Time to get creative!

INGREDIENTS

2 cups of Peanut Butter Chex (or your favorite cereal)
1 cup peanuts
½ cup almonds
½ cup walnuts
½ cup pumpkin seeds
½ cup chocolate chips
½ cup dried cranberries

NUTRITION FACTS (per serving)

Calories: 335
Carbs: 30g
Protein: 11g
Fat: 27g
Fiber: 6g

DIRECTIONS

1. Combine all ingredients in a large bowl.

2. Store in a covered airtight container, or place in individual baggies for an easy grab-and-go snack option. Trail mix will keep for up to 1 month when stored in a cool and dark place.

SWAPS

Gluten-Free
Use gluten-free cereal

Dairy-Free
Use dairy-free chocolate chips and cereal

Vegan/Vegetarian
Recipe is already vegetarian. If vegan, use dairy-free chocolate chips and cereal

Crispy Chickpeas

45 MINUTES • SERVES 6

Sometimes you need to shake up your snack routine, and crispy chickpeas can help you do just that. You can also use these as an ingredient in recipes like the Roasted Chickpea Gyros on page 61, but I personally like grabbing a handful as a snack. Feel free to try a different combination of spices in order to change up the flavor over and over again.

INGREDIENTS

1 (15.5-ounce) can chickpeas, drained
1 tablespoon olive oil
½ teaspoon paprika
½ teaspoon oregano
½ teaspoon garlic powder
½ teaspoon cumin
Pinch of salt
Pinch of black pepper
Pinch of red pepper flakes, optional

NUTRITION FACTS (per serving)

Calories: 101
Carbs: 14g
Protein: 4g
Fat: 4g
Fiber: 4g

DIRECTIONS

1. Preheat oven to 375°F and line a small baking sheet with parchment paper.

2. Pat chickpeas dry with a kitchen towel and spread out in one even layer on the baking sheet. Bake for 30 minutes.

3. Toss chickpeas with oil and spices, then bake for an additional 10 minutes. Cool and store in an airtight container at room temperature for up to 1 week.

SWAPS

Gluten-Free
Recipe is already gluten-free

Dairy-Free
Recipe is already dairy-free

Vegan/Vegetarian
Recipe is already vegan

Hummus Jars

5 MINUTES • SERVES 4

How many times have you bought vegetables for a snack only to find them left uneaten at the end of the week? Meal prep these hummus jars and make snack time fun. Now you'll have a reason to grab those veggies you bought. Feel free to make your own hummus (see page 103), or use whatever brand you prefer or whatever's on sale.

INGREDIENTS

1 ⅓ cups hummus
2 carrots, cut into 3-inch sticks
4 celery stalks, cut into 3-inch sticks

NUTRITION FACTS (per serving)
Calories: 212
Carbs: 16g
Protein: 7g
Fat: 15g
Fiber: 6g

DIRECTIONS

1. Spoon ⅓ cup hummus into the bottom of each of four 2-cup glass containers. Divide the carrots and celery equally among the containers.

2. Refrigerate in covered airtight containers until ready to eat, for up to 5 days.

SWAPS

Gluten-Free
Recipe is already gluten-free

Dairy-Free
Recipe is already dairy-free

Vegan/Vegetarian
Recipe is already vegan

No-Bake Protein Bars

15 MINUTES • SERVES 8

You can certainly buy premade protein bars, and I'm not discouraging you from doing so. However, sometimes you have all the ingredients you need at home and could save a buck or two by making your own. These are best if left in the freezer, so take them out when you are ready to eat them or make sure to pack in a cooler bag if you're packing them for lunch.

INGREDIENTS

1 cup creamy peanut butter
½ cup protein powder (vanilla or chocolate)
¼ cup maple syrup
1 teaspoon vanilla extract
Pinch of salt
⅓ cup chocolate chips

NUTRITION FACTS (per serving)

Calories: 302
Carbs: 20g
Protein: 13g
Fat: 20g
Fiber: 2g

DIRECTIONS

1. Line an 8-x-8-inch baking dish with parchment paper.

2. Blend peanut butter, protein powder, maple syrup, vanilla extract, and salt in a blender or food processor until smooth. Fold in chocolate chips.

3. Press mixture into an even layer in the prepared pan. Place in the freezer for 10 minutes.

4. Slice into 8 bars and store in an airtight container in the freezer for up to 3 months.

SWAPS

Gluten-Free

Recipe is already gluten-free

Dairy-Free

Use a plant-based or egg-based protein powder and use dairy-free chocolate chips

Vegan/Vegetarian

Recipe is already vegetarian. If vegan, use a plant-based protein powder and dairy-free chocolate chips

Creamy Avocado Dip

5 MINUTES • SERVES 4

I love guacamole, but every once in a while, I like to change it up. This creamy avocado dip has a tangy punch and a nice creaminess to it thanks to the yogurt. Pack it with your lunch and pair with sliced vegetables, or use it to top your tacos.

INGREDIENTS

1 avocado
Juice of ½ lime
⅓ cup plain Greek yogurt
Salt and pepper, to taste

NUTRITION FACTS (per serving)

Calories: 97
Carbs: 6g
Protein: 3g
Fat: 8g
Fiber: 3g

DIRECTIONS

1. In a small bowl, mash avocado with lime juice with the back of a fork.

2. Stir in yogurt until well combined.

3. Season with salt and pepper as desired.

4. Serve with tortilla chips, or store in an airtight container in the refrigerator for up to 3 days.

SWAPS

Gluten-Free
Recipe is already gluten-free

Dairy-Free
Use dairy-free yogurt

Vegan/Vegetarian
Recipe is already vegetarian.
If vegan, use dairy-free yogurt

Energy Bites

30 MINUTES • SERVES 12

I'm always looking for snacks that I can make ahead of time and just grab quickly during my busy workday. These energy bites are one of my favorites to make and to eat. I love to double or triple the batch and keep them in the freezer for a few months.

INGREDIENTS

1 cup rolled oats
⅔ cup nut butter
⅓ cup chocolate chips
3 tablespoons honey
Pinch of salt

NUTRITION FACTS (per serving)

Calories: 166
Carbs: 16g
Protein: 4g
Fat: 10g
Fiber: 1g

DIRECTIONS

1. In a medium bowl, combine all ingredients and stir until well mixed.

2. Roll into golf ball–sized balls and place on a baking sheet. Freeze for 20 minutes, or until set.

3. Store in an airtight container in the refrigerator for 1 week or in the freezer for up to 3 months. If frozen, you can eat directly from the freezer or thaw for a few minutes, depending on your preference.

SWAPS

Gluten-Free
Use certified gluten-free oats

Dairy-Free
Use dairy-free chocolate chips

Vegan/Vegetarian
Recipe is already vegetarian. If vegan, use maple syrup in place of honey and dairy-free chocolate chips

Rice Cakes Three Ways

5 MINUTES • EACH VARIETY SERVES 1

I love rice cakes, not for the rice cakes themselves, but because they are the perfect vehicle for a filling snack. You can turn them into a sweet or savory snack and can easily change up the flavors based on what you have on hand. Here are three of my favorite ways to enjoy rice cakes, but feel free to get creative.

Peanut Butter & Apple

INGREDIENTS

1 plain rice cake
1 ½ tablespoons peanut butter
½ apple, sliced
Pinch of cinnamon

DIRECTIONS

1. Spread peanut butter on rice cake. Top with apple and cinnamon.

2. Enjoy immediately.

NUTRITION FACTS (per serving)
Calories: 226
Carbs: 25g
Protein: 6g
Fat: 13g
Fiber: 4g

Hummus and Cucumber

INGREDIENTS

1 plain rice cake
2 tablespoons hummus
3 to 4 slices cucumber
Pinch of paprika

DIRECTIONS

1. Spread hummus on rice cake. Top with cucumber and paprika.

2. Enjoy immediately.

NUTRITION FACTS (per serving)
Calories: 119
Carbs: 15g
Protein: 3g
Fat: 6g
Fiber: 3g

Greek Yogurt and Berries

INGREDIENTS

1 plain rice cake
2 tablespoons plain Greek yogurt
⅓ cup berries
1 teaspoon honey

DIRECTIONS

1. Spread yogurt on rice cake. Top with berries and honey.

2. Enjoy immediately.

NUTRITION FACTS (per serving)

Calories: 106
Carbs: 22g
Protein: 4g
Fat: 1g
Fiber: 2g

SWAPS

Gluten-Free
Recipe is already gluten-free

Dairy-Free
Use dairy-free yogurt

Vegan/Vegetarian
Recipe is already vegetarian.
If vegan, use dairy-free yogurt and maple syrup instead of honey

Cottage Cheese Cups

5 MINUTES • EACH VARIETY SERVES 1

Snacks don't have to be complicated to get the job done. These snacks are simple yet filling. I gave you two versions because sometimes you're in the mood for a savory snack, and sometimes you feel like something a little sweeter. So now you have options, and don't we all love options?!

Savory

INGREDIENTS

½ cup cottage cheese
1 hard-boiled egg (page 104)
6 slices cucumber
6 cherry tomatoes, halved
Salt and pepper, to taste

DIRECTIONS

1. Place cottage cheese in a small bowl and top with hard-boiled egg, cucumber, cherry tomatoes, salt, and pepper.

2. Enjoy immediately.

NUTRITION FACTS (per serving)

Calories: 196
Carbs: 9g
Protein: 19g
Fat: 9g
Fiber: 1g

Sweet

INGREDIENTS

½ cup cottage cheese
1 tablespoon peanut butter
1 tablespoon jelly
¼ cup berries

DIRECTIONS

1. Place cottage cheese in a small bowl and top with peanut butter, jelly, and berries.

2. Enjoy immediately.

NUTRITION FACTS (per serving)

Calories: 270
Carbs: 25g
Protein: 16g
Fat: 13g
Fiber: 2g

SWAPS

Gluten-Free
Recipe is already gluten-free

Dairy-Free
Use a dairy-free yogurt in place of cottage cheese

Vegan/Vegetarian
Recipe is already vegetarian. If vegan, use a dairy-free yogurt in place of cottage cheese; omit egg

Edible Cookie Dough Dip

10 MINUTES • SERVES 8

Who doesn't love eating cookie dough while making cookies? This snack was inspired by standard cookie dough, but is made with chickpeas and no raw egg. Feel free to eat it with a spoon.

INGREDIENTS

1 (15.5-ounce) can chickpeas, drained
⅓ cup peanut butter
1 tablespoon maple syrup
1 tablespoon milk of choice
½ teaspoon vanilla extract
¼ cup chocolate chips
Pinch of salt

NUTRITION FACTS (per serving)

Calories: 176
Carbs: 18g
Protein: 6g
Fat: 9g
Fiber: 3g

DIRECTIONS

1. Blend chickpeas, peanut butter, maple syrup, milk, and vanilla extract in a food processor or blender until smooth.

2. Fold in chocolate chips and add a pinch of salt.

3. Serve with graham crackers, fruit, or pretzels for dipping, or store in an airtight container in the refrigerator for up to 5 days.

SWAPS

Gluten-Free
Recipe is already gluten-free

Dairy-Free
Use dairy-free milk and chocolate chips

Vegan/Vegetarian
Recipe is already vegetarian.
If vegan, use dairy-free milk and dairy-free chocolate chips

Healthy No-Bake Cookies

30 MINUTES • SERVES 16

I am not a baker, but I still like a sweet snack once in a while. So if I can satisfy my sweet tooth without having to bake, it's a win-win. Use your favorite protein powder for this recipe: I've used vanilla, chocolate, and cinnamon, but feel free to change up the flavor and use whatever you have on hand.

INGREDIENTS

½ cup melted coconut oil
½ cup peanut butter
2 ½ cups rolled oats
½ cup protein powder
½ cup chocolate chips
¼ cup maple syrup
2 tablespoons milk of choice
1 teaspoon vanilla extract
Pinch of salt

NUTRITION FACTS (per serving)

Calories: 226
Carbs: 18g
Protein: 6g
Fat: 14g
Fiber: 2g

DIRECTIONS

1. In a large bowl, whisk together coconut oil and peanut butter. Add remaining ingredients and stir to combine.

2. Drop spoonfuls of dough onto a parchment-lined baking sheet and place in the freezer for 20 minutes, or until set.

3. Store in an airtight container in the refrigerator for up to 1 week or in the freezer for up to 1 month.

SWAPS

Gluten-Free
Use gluten-free oats

Dairy-Free
Use dairy-free milk, a plant-based protein powder, and dairy-free chocolate chips

Vegan/Vegetarian
Recipe is already vegetarian.
If vegan, use dairy-free milk, a plant-based protein powder, and dairy-free chocolate chips

Basics

Simple White Rice

30 MINUTES • SERVES 4

INGREDIENTS

1 cup long-grain white rice
2 cups water or broth
Pinch of salt

NUTRITION FACTS (per serving)

Calories: 160
Carbs: 38g
Protein: 3g
Fat: 0g
Fiber: 1g

DIRECTIONS

1. In a medium saucepan, combine rice, water, and salt and bring to a boil.

2. Cover, turn heat down to low, and cook for 20 minutes.

3. Remove from the heat and allow to sit for 5 minutes, then fluff with a fork before serving.

4. Enjoy immediately or store in an airtight container in the refrigerator for up to 3 days.

Homemade Hummus

5 MINUTES • SERVES 8 (yields about 1 ½ cups)

INGREDIENTS

1 (15-ounce) can chickpeas, drained
¼ cup tahini
2 tablespoons water, plus more as needed
2 tablespoons olive oil
Juice of 1 lemon
2 cloves garlic
½ teaspoon paprika
Salt and pepper, to taste

NUTRITION FACTS (per serving)

Calories:164
Carbs: 17g
Protein: 6g
Fat: 9g
Fiber: 5g

DIRECTIONS

1. Combine all ingredients in a food processor or blender and blend on high until smooth.

2. Enjoy immediately or store in an airtight container in the refrigerator for up to 1 week.

Taco Seasoning

5 MINUTES • Yields 4 tablespoons

INGREDIENTS

2 tablespoons chili powder

1 teaspoon cumin

1 teaspoon oregano

1 teaspoon garlic powder

1 teaspoon onion powder

1 teaspoon paprika

1 teaspoon salt

½ teaspoon black pepper

NUTRITION FACTS (per serving)

Calories:15

Carbs: 3g

Protein: 1g

Fat: 1g

Fiber: 1g

DIRECTIONS

1. Combine all seasonings in a medium bowl.

2. Store in an airtight container for up to 1 year.

Hard-Boiled Eggs

30 MINUTES • SERVES 8

INGREDIENTS

8 large eggs

NUTRITION FACTS (per serving)

Calories: 72

Carbs: 0g

Protein: 6g

Fat: 5g

Fiber: 0g

DIRECTIONS

1. Place eggs in a single layer on the bottom of a large pot. Add enough cold water to cover eggs by about 1 inch.

2. Place over high heat and bring to a boil, then immediately turn the heat off, cover, and let sit for 10 minutes.

3. Meanwhile, fill a bowl with ice water. After 10 minutes, transfer eggs to the ice bath and let sit for another 10 minutes.

4. Peel eggs and enjoy immediately, or store unpeeled in the refrigerator for up to 5 days.

Easy Baked Chicken

35 MINUTES • SERVES 4

INGREDIENTS

2 chicken breasts (about 1 pound)
1 tablespoon olive oil
½ teaspoon salt
¼ teaspoon black pepper

NUTRITION FACTS (per serving)
Calories: 166
Carbs: 0g
Protein: 25g
Fat: 6g
Fiber: 0g

DIRECTIONS

1. Preheat oven to 400°F.

2. Place chicken breasts in a single layer in a baking dish. Drizzle with olive oil and sprinkle evenly with salt and pepper.

3. Bake for 25 minutes, or until internal temperature reaches 165°F.

4. Let rest for 5 minutes, then slice and serve as desired, or store in an airtight container in the refrigerator for up to 5 days.

Simple Ground Meat

15 MINUTES • SERVES 4

INGREDIENTS

2 teaspoons olive oil
1 pound lean ground meat (beef, turkey, chicken, etc.)
Salt and pepper, to taste

NUTRITION FACTS (per serving)
Calories: 220
Carbs: 0g
Protein: 23g
Fat: 14g
Fiber: 0g

DIRECTIONS

1. Heat oil in a medium skillet over medium-high heat.

2. Add meat and break up into small pieces, then let cook for 4 to 5 minutes without touching.

3. Stir meat for about 6-7 minutes and continue to cook until meat is no longer pink.

4. Add salt and pepper and stir to coat evenly. Serve immediately or store in an airtight container in the refrigerator for up to 1 week.

Roasted Vegetables

60 MINUTES • SERVES 4

INGREDIENTS

2 tablespoons olive oil

4 medium red potatoes, chopped

1 head of broccoli, chopped

1 red bell pepper, chopped

1 red onion, chopped

4 cloves garlic, minced

Salt and pepper, to taste

NUTRITION FACTS (per serving)

Calories: 194

Carbs: 31g

Protein: 5g

Fat: 7g

Fiber: 5g

DIRECTIONS

1. Preheat oven to 425°F and line a baking sheet with parchment paper.

2. In a large bowl, toss potatoes, broccoli, bell pepper, and onion with olive oil. Mix in garlic and toss so that all vegetables are evenly coated, but not drenched.

3. Spread vegetables onto the prepared baking sheet in a single layer. Bake for 40 to 50 minutes, or until tender.

4. Season with salt and pepper and enjoy immediately, or store in the refrigerator for up to 1 week.

Marinara Sauce

15 MINUTES • SERVES 4

INGREDIENTS

1 tablespoon olive oil

1 yellow onion, diced

1 green bell pepper, diced

3 cloves garlic, minced

1 (28-ounce) can whole peeled tomatoes

½ cup water

2 teaspoons parsley

2 teaspoons oregano

½ teaspoon salt

¼ teaspoon black pepper

NUTRITION FACTS (per serving)

Calories: 92 calories

Carbs: 13g

Protein: 2g

Fat: 0g

Fiber: 3g

DIRECTIONS

1. Heat oil in a large saucepan over medium heat. Add onion and bell pepper and cook, stirring for 2 minutes, then add garlic and cook for another minute.

2. Stir in tomatoes, water, parsley, oregano, salt, and pepper, and cook on low for 5 minutes, stirring frequently.

3. Remove from heat and, using an immersion blender, blend on high until smooth (or carefully pour mixture into a blender or food processor to blend). Return to heat and keep heated on low until ready to serve.

Cheat
Sheets

Pantry Staples

This is not an exhaustive list, but keeping some or all of these foods on hand in your pantry is a good way to make meal planning and meal prepping easier. I suggest making a note of the ones you use often, so that when you are meal planning you can refer back to this list and take a quick peek in your kitchen to see which staples you may need to restock. It's a good idea to stock up on the shelf-stable ingredients ahead of time, so you always have food on hand when the leftovers run out.

Fats & Oils

Avocados
Avocado oil
Butter
Coconut (shredded)
Coconut oil
Extra-virgin olive oil
Full-fat coconut milk (canned)
Ghee/clarified butter
Olives
Sesame oil

Grains

Oats
Pasta
Quinoa
Rice: basmati, jasmine, brown, etc.

Herbs & Spices

Black pepper
Chili powder
Cinnamon
Cumin
Garlic powder
Onion powder
Paprika
Red pepper flakes
Salt
Turmeric

Legumes (canned or dried)

Black beans
Chickpeas
Kidney beans
Lentils
Pinto beans

Nuts & Seeds

Almonds
Brazil nuts
Cashews
Chestnuts
Hazelnuts
Macadamia nuts
Nut butters (unsweetened and natural)
Peanuts
Pistachios
Pumpkin seeds
Sesame seeds
Sunflower seeds
Walnuts

Other

Broth (beef, chicken, and vegetable)
Canned fish: salmon, sardines, tuna, etc.
Coconut aminos (a great gluten-free substitute for soy sauce)
Diced tomatoes (canned)
Dried fruit (unsweetened)
Cocoa powder
Hot sauce
Mustard
Pumpkin (canned)
Soy sauce and/or tamari
Tomato paste
Tomato sauce (unsweetened)
Vinegars: apple cider, balsamic, distilled, red wine, etc.

Using Leftovers

Leftovers make for easy meal planning. While you can certainly just reheat leftover food and serve it as-is, sometimes the same thing over and over again can get boring. Here are a few fun ways to use leftovers as the starting point for a whole new meal.

- Make anything a salad by topping a bowl of greens with leftovers

- Make anything a bowl by combining a grain, a veggie, and a meat. Have leftover ground meat? Make some rice or quinoa and roast some veggies. Put it all in a bowl, top with your favorite dressing, and dinner is served

- Make an omelet. If you have leftover veggies or meat, heat them in a skillet over medium heat, add 2- to 3 whisked eggs, and add your spices of choice: Instant breakfast for dinner!

- Blend leftover fruit into a smoothie bowl for any meal or snack

- Dip leftover veggies in hummus or top a rice cake with them for a midday snack

- Put an egg on it. This is a personal favorite of mine—when you have leftovers, but not as much as you'd like, just add an egg cooked any way you like to beef up your meal

- Make a wrap or burrito. Heat up your random leftovers and serve them in a tortilla with your favorite sauce, dip, or cheese

When all else fails, freeze your leftovers if you don't think you'll eat them within 2 to 3 days, so that you can enjoy them later. I recommend freezing them in whatever portion size you plan to serve them in eventually.

Freezer Storage

Using your freezer can help make meal prep and planning easier. We don't always have time to plan or prep ahead (think about going away on vacation and coming home to an empty fridge on Sunday night). And sometimes we run out of food even when we do plan ahead. In these moments, having a fully stocked freezer can help keep you on track, so that you don't have to run out to the store or order takeout.

FREEZER ESSENTIALS

Having food in the freezer does not make you lazy; it makes you prepared. A well-stocked freezer can help you pull together a great last-minute emergency meal or snack. Some of my favorite essentials to keep on hand include:

- **FROZEN FRUIT**
  berries, mangoes, peaches

- **FROZEN FISH**
  salmon, shrimp, cod or other white fish

- **FROZEN MEAT**
  ground beef, ground turkey, chicken breasts

- **FROZEN VEGGIES**
  spinach, broccoli, cauliflower rice, corn, bell pepper

- **LEFTOVER INGREDIENTS**
  tomato paste, canned pumpkin, pesto, etc.

You can also precook full meals or snacks to keep in the freezer for busy nights. Recipes in this book that freeze well include:

- Make-Ahead Freezer Burritos (page 31)

- Egg Cups Five Ways (page 41)

- Slow Cooker Chili (page 65)

- Turkey Stuffed Peppers (page 70)

- Energy Bites (page 93)

- No-Bake Protein Bars (page 89)

- Healthy No-Bake Cookies (page 100)

Unfortunately, some foods do not hold up well to freezing. While it would be nice to be able to freeze everything, some things are just better fresh. Do not freeze any of the following:

- Lettuce and greens

- Celery

- Cucumbers

- Tomatoes

- Cooked pasta or rice

- Hard-boiled eggs

HOW LONG CAN YOU FREEZE FOOD?

Most food can be frozen for quite a while, but if it's not properly wrapped or has been frozen for too long, the first sign will often be freezer burn. To extend the life of your frozen food, make sure it is wrapped tightly in plastic wrap and then in a freezer-safe storage bag or container, so that there is little or no exposure to air.

I recommend freezing food in single-serving quantities so it's easy to reheat what you need later on. Make sure to mark the date on the packaging before you put food in the freezer so you know how old it is. If you notice freezer burn, or if the food is

past the recommended freezing time, unfortunately it may be best to discard it. Here's a general guideline for how long you can keep most frozen foods:

- **FRESH HERBS**
  12 months

- **FRUIT**
  6 to 12 months

- **PRE-COOKED FOOD/LEFTOVERS**
  3 to 4 months

- **RAW FISH**
  3 to 6 months

- **RAW MEAT**
  12 months

- **VEGETABLES**
  6 to 12 months

Storing Fresh Fruits and Vegetables

It's great that you want to add more fruits and vegetables to your meal plan, but it can be so frustrating when you go to use a fresh item and it's spoiled. Here are a few tips for keeping your produce fresh for longer.

- **POTATOES**
  Do not refrigerate, but store in a dark, cool place away from items like onions and bananas.

- **ONIONS AND GARLIC**
  Do not refrigerate, but store in a dark, cool place away from potatoes.

- **LEAFY GREENS**
  Either store unwashed in a plastic bag, or wash and dry thoroughly and place in a large plastic storage container lined with paper towels. If you buy pre-washed greens, you can leave them sealed in the bag they came in for up to five days. If you plan on letting them sit in your fridge longer, though, follow the rules for loose leafy greens.

- **APPLES AND PEARS**
  Store in the refrigerator in a plastic bag

- **CITRUS FRUIT**
  Store on the counter for up to one week, or loose in the refrigerator for two weeks or more.

- **BROCCOLI/CAULIFLOWER**
  Store in the refrigerator in a sealed container.

- **BERRIES**
  Do not wash until ready to eat. Store in an airtight container lined with paper towels.

- **MUSHROOMS**
  Store in a paper bag in the refrigerator.

- **CELERY**
  Wrap in aluminum foil and keep in the refrigerator.

- **AVOCADO**
  Allow to ripen on your countertop. Once fully ripe, store in the refrigerator until ready to eat.

- **TOMATOES**
  Store at room temperature in a bowl with plenty of room, away from the sun or heat.

Avoiding Waste

Sometimes we don't need the whole fruit, vegetable, or herb we've purchased, and it can be frustrating to throw out what we don't use. Here are a few ways I like to use the extras.

- **CITRUS FRUITS**
  If you're only using the juice or fruit itself, zest the skins using a zester or fine cheese grater before you cut it, and store the zest in an airtight container in the refrigerator to use as a topping on dishes like the Carne Asada Tacos or Yogurt Parfaits.

- **BANANAS**
  If they start turning brown before you can use them, peel and chop them and store in the freezer in an airtight container or bag to use later for smoothies or smoothie bowls.

- **STEMS AND TRIMMINGS FROM ONIONS, PEPPERS, BROCCOLI, ETC.**
  Store these in an airtight bag in the freezer to use whenever you're making a broth or a stock.

- **EXTRA HERBS**
  Puree with olive oil and parmesan cheese in a blender or food processor to make pesto.

- **OVERRIPE BERRIES**
  To make berry jam, combine with sugar and lemon juice in a saucepan and cook over medium heat for 15 minutes, stirring frequently until it forms a gel.

- **TOMATO PASTE**
  Spoon into an ice cube tray, placing 1 to 2 tablespoons in each well, and freeze. When completely frozen, remove from the ice cube tray and store in a freezer-safe bag to use in chilis, tomato sauces, etc.

Additional Resources

While I hope this book is a one-stop shop for all of your meal-planning and prep needs, once you get started, you may want to learn even more. The following resources will elevate your cooking with more recipe ideas and information meal planning and preparation.

- **THE SASSY DIETITIAN**
  thesassydietitian.com
  This is my website, where you can find more information on meal planning and prep as well as even more easy recipes.

- **THE KITCHN**
  thekitchn.com
  This website is chock-full of resources for meal planning, prepping, and cooking techniques. You can also find easy recipes and step-by-step instructions for how to cook single ingredients.

- **BUDGET BYTES**
  budgetbytes.com
  This website has so many easy-to-meal-prep recipes, as well as guides for meal prepping on a budget.

- **AMERICA'S TEST KITCHEN**
  americastestkitchen.com
  Ever wish you had an expert to stand behind you and guide you in the kitchen? This is your go-to resource for all things food, ingredients, and recipes. It's never too late to start learning new skills.

- **MONTEREY BAY AQUARIUM'S SEAFOOD WATCH GUIDE**
  seafoodwatch.org
  A resource to help you better understand your choices when it comes to seafood and seafood quality. You can stay up to date on which fish are best for consumption as well as which fish may be high in things like mercury.

About the Author

LAURA LIGOS, MBA, RDN, CSSD, is an Albany, NY-based sports dietitian and online real food-based blogger, educator, and nutrition expert. She received her Bachelor of Science degree in Nutrition Sciences from Cornell University. She went on to complete her Dietetic Internship and Master of Business Administration at Dominican University.

As a lifelong athlete, she went on to pursue many ventures as a dietitian, but knew her passion was in sports nutrition and teaching people how to cook and build a real-food lifestyle. Today, she educates people in her hometown as well as through her blog at thesassydietitian.com and on her Instagram account, @thesassydietitian.

Ligos currently resides in Albany, NY, with her husband, son, and Wheaten Terrier pup.

Sample Meal Plans

The next few pages provide you with a few sample meal plans to help get you started on your journey. You can follow these plans as you get started, or use them more as a guide to help you better understand what a typical week might look like. Each of these plans was designed with an average 2,000-calorie day in mind, however you can remove a snack or scale up or down the other recipes to meet your individual goals.

Week 1 ~~~~~~~~~~

MONDAY
Breakfast: Homemade Yogurt Parfait
Lunch: Turkey Hummus Sandwich and Baby Carrots
Dinner: Shrimp Stir-Fry and Quinoa
Snacks: Edible Cookie Dough Dip and Apple;
Homemade Trail Mix; PB and Apple Rice Cake

TUESDAY
Breakfast: Homemade Yogurt Parfait
Lunch: Turkey Hummus Sandwich and Baby Carrots
Dinner: Shrimp Stir-Fry and Quinoa
Snacks: Edible Cookie Dough Dip and Apple;
Homemade Trail Mix; PB and Apple Rice Cake

WEDNESDAY
Breakfast: Protein Pancakes and Blueberries
Lunch: Turkey Hummus Sandwich and Baby Carrots
Dinner: Turkey Stuffed Peppers
Snacks: Grapes; Homemade Trail Mix; PB & Apple
Rice Cake

THURSDAY
Breakfast: Protein Pancakes and Blueberries
Lunch: Out to lunch
Dinner: Turkey Stuffed Peppers
Snacks: Grapes; Homemade Trail Mix; PB & Apple
Rice Cake

FRIDAY
Breakfast: Protein Pancakes and Blueberries
Lunch: Bento Box: Tuna Salad
Dinner: Out to Dinner
Snacks: Cottage Cheese Cup (Savory); Homemade
Trail Mix; PB & Apple Rice Cake

SATURDAY
Breakfast: Protein Pancakes and Blueberries
Lunch: Bento Box: Tuna Salad
Dinner: One-Skillet Chicken Fajitas and White Rice
Snacks: Cottage Cheese Cup (Savory); Homemade
Trail Mix; PB & Apple Rice Cake

SUNDAY
Breakfast: BYO Smoothie Bowl
Lunch: Bento Box: Tuna Salad
Dinner: One-Skillet Chicken Fajitas and White Rice
Snacks: Cottage Cheese Cup (Savory); Homemade
Trail Mix; PB & Apple Rice Cake

Week 2

MONDAY

Breakfast: 2 Mushroom, Pepper, and Spinach Egg Cups
Lunch: Bento Box: Hummus Veggie Wrap
Dinner: Lentil Tortilla Soup
Snacks: No-Bake Protein Bar; Grapes and Cashews; Yogurt and Berries Rice Cake

TUESDAY

Breakfast: 2 Mushroom, Pepper, and Spinach Egg Cups
Lunch: Bento Box: Hummus Veggie Wrap
Dinner: Lentil Tortilla Soup
Snacks: No-Bake Protein Bar; Grapes and Cashews; Yogurt and Berries Rice Cake

WEDNESDAY

Breakfast: 2 Mushroom, Pepper, and Spinach Egg Cups
Lunch: Bento Box: Hummus Veggie Wrap
Dinner: Lentil Tortilla Soup
Snacks: No-Bake Protein Bar; Grapes and Cashews; Yogurt and Berries Rice Cake

THURSDAY

Breakfast: Apple Cinnamon Baked Oatmeal
Lunch: Lentil Tortilla Soup
Dinner: One-Pot Taco Pasta
Snacks: No-Bake Protein Bar; Banana; Yogurt and Berries Rice Cake

FRIDAY

Breakfast: Apple Cinnamon Baked Oatmeal
Lunch: Lentil Tortilla Soup
Dinner: One-Pot Taco Pasta
Snacks: No-Bake Protein Bar; Banana; Yogurt and Berries Rice Cake

SATURDAY

Breakfast: BYO Smoothie Bowl
Lunch: Lentil Tortilla Soup
Dinner: Out to dinner
Snacks: No-Bake Protein Bar; Banana; Yogurt and Berries Rice Cake

SUNDAY

Breakfast: BYO Smoothie Bowl
Lunch: Bento Box: Hummus Veggie Wrap
Dinner: One-Pot Taco Pasta
Snacks: No-Bake Protein Bar; Banana; Yogurt and Berries Rice Cake

Week 3

MONDAY
Breakfast: Make-Ahead Freezer Burrito
Lunch: Bento Box: Turkey and Cheese
Dinner: Roasted Chickpea Gyros
Snacks: Healthy No-Bake Cookies; Cottage Cheese
Cup (sweet); Energy Bites

TUESDAY
Breakfast: Make-Ahead Freezer Burrito
Lunch: Bento Box: Turkey and Cheese
Dinner: Roasted Chickpea Gyros
Snacks: Healthy No-Bake Cookies; Cottage Cheese
Cup (sweet) ; Energy Bites

WEDNESDAY
Breakfast: Make-Ahead Freezer Burrito
Lunch: Roasted Chickpea Gyros
Dinner: Sheet Pan Teriyaki Chicken and Veggies
Snacks: Healthy No-Bake Cookies; Homemade
Yogurt Parfait; Energy Bites

THURSDAY
Breakfast: Make-Ahead Freezer Burrito
Lunch: Roasted Chickpea Gyros
Dinner: Sheet Pan Teriyaki Chicken and Veggies
Snacks: Healthy No-Bake Cookies; Homemade
Yogurt Parfait; Energy Bites

FRIDAY
Breakfast: PB&J Overnight Oats
Lunch: Salmon Salad Lettuce Wraps and Clementine
Dinner: Out to dinner
Snacks: Healthy No-Bake Cookies; Hummus Jars;
Energy Bites

SATURDAY
Breakfast: PB&J Overnight Oats
Lunch: Salmon Salad Lettuce Wraps and Clementine
Dinner: Mongolian Beef Ramen
Snacks: Healthy No-Bake Cookies; Hummus Jars;
Energy Bites

SUNDAY
Breakfast: PB&J Overnight Oats
Lunch: Salmon Salad Lettuce Wraps and Clementine
Dinner: Mongolian Beef Ramen
Snacks: Healthy No-Bake Cookies; Hummus Jars;
Energy Bites

Week 4 (vegetarian)

MONDAY

Breakfast: Chocolate PB Cup Overnight Oats
Lunch: Bento Box: Hard-Boiled Eggs
Dinner: Lentil Tortilla Soup
Snacks: Homemade Trail Mix; Crispy Chickpeas;
Apple with Almond Butter

TUESDAY

Breakfast: Chocolate PB Cup Overnight Oats
Lunch: Bento Box: Hard-Boiled Eggs
Dinner: Lentil Tortilla Soup
Snacks: Homemade Trail Mix; Crispy Chickpeas;
Apple with Almond Butter

WEDNESDAY

Breakfast: Chocolate PB Cup Overnight Oats
Lunch: Lentil Tortilla Soup
Dinner: Sesame Tofu Quinoa Bowls
Snacks: Homemade Trail Mix; Crispy Chickpeas;
PB & Apple Rice Cake

THURSDAY

Breakfast: Chocolate PB Cup Overnight Oats
Lunch: Strawberry Goat Cheese Salad
Dinner: Sesame Tofu Quinoa Bowls
Snacks: Homemade Trail Mix; Crispy Chickpeas;
PB & Apple Rice Cake

FRIDAY

Breakfast: 2 Kale, Mushroom, and Swiss Egg Cups
Lunch: Out to lunch
Dinner: Mushroom and Veggie Tacos and White Rice
Snacks: Homemade Trail Mix; Crispy Chickpeas;
Banana with Almond Butter

SATURDAY

Breakfast: 2 Kale, Mushroom, and Swiss Egg Cups
Lunch: Strawberry Goat Cheese Salad
Dinner: Mushroom and Veggie Tacos and White Rice
Snacks: Homemade Trail Mix; Crispy Chickpeas;
Banana with Almond Butter

SUNDAY

Breakfast: 2 Kale, Mushroom, and Swiss Egg Cups
Lunch: Strawberry Goat Cheese Salad
Dinner: Out to dinner
Snacks: Homemade Trail Mix; Apple